T0270642

Journalism Design

'*Journalism Design* wrestles with fundamental questions of how journalism should respond to changing technology and human behaviour. It focuses on improving understanding of how users acquire and interact with news in the digital world and how news organisations can better design that experience. Classic journalism storytelling and presentation were dictated by the needs of the telegraph and typesetting equipment. Skye Doherty offers prototypes that reveal intriguing new approaches for improving contemporary value and fostering effective news delivery with digital technologies.'

– Robert G. Picard, Professor, Reuters Institute
for the Study of Journalism, University of Oxford, UK

Journalism Design is about the future of journalism. As technologies increasingly, and continually, reshape the way we interact with information, with each other and with our environment, journalists need new ways to tell stories.

Journalists often see technology as something that improves what they are doing or that makes it more convenient. However, the growing might of technology companies has put journalism and news organisations in a difficult position: readers and revenues have moved, and platforms exert increasing control over story design. Skye Doherty argues that, rather than adapting journalism to new technologies, journalists should be creating the technologies themselves and those technologies should be designed for core values such as the public interest. Drawing from theories and practices of interaction design, this book demonstrates how journalists can use their expertise to imagine new ways of doing journalism. The design and development of the NewsCube, a three-dimensional storytelling tool, is detailed, as well as how interaction design can be used to imagine new forms of journalism. The book concludes by calling for closer ties between researchers and working journalists and suggests that journalism has a hybrid future – in newsrooms, communities, design studios and tech companies.

Skye Doherty is a lecturer in Journalism at the University of Queensland's School of Communication and Arts. Her research and teaching straddle journalism and interaction design.

Disruptions: Studies in Digital Journalism
Series editor: Bob Franklin

For a full list of titles in this series, please visit:
www.routledge.com/Disruptions/book-series/DISRUPTDIGJOUR

Disruptions refers to the radical changes provoked by the affordances of digital technologies that occur at a pace and on a scale that disrupts settled understandings and traditional ways of creating value, interacting and communicating both socially and professionally. The consequences for digital journalism involve far-reaching changes to business models, professional practices, roles, ethics, products and even challenges to the accepted definitions and understandings of journalism. For Digital Journalism Studies, the field of academic inquiry which explores and examines digital journalism, disruption results in paradigmatic and tectonic shifts in scholarly concerns and prompts reconsideration of research methods, theoretical analyses and responses (oppositional and consensual) to such changes, which have been described as being akin to 'a moment of mind blowing uncertainty'.

Routledge's new book series, *Disruptions: Studies in Digital Journalism*, seeks to capture, examine and analyse these moments of exciting and explosive professional and scholarly innovation which characterise developments in the day-to-day practice of journalism in an age of digital media and which are articulated in the newly emerging academic discipline of Digital Journalism Studies.

Fake News: Falsehood, Fabrication and Fantasy in Journalism
Brian McNair

Journalism Design: Interactive Technologies and the Future of Storytelling
Skye Doherty

Journalism Design
Interactive Technologies
and the Future of Storytelling

Skye Doherty

Routledge
Taylor & Francis Group

LONDON AND NEW YORK

First published 2018 by Routledge

2 Park Square, Milton Park, Abingdon, Oxon OX14 4RN
605 Third Avenue, New York, NY 10017

Routledge is an imprint of the Taylor & Francis Group, an informa business

First issued in paperback 2021

British Library Cataloguing-in-Publication Data
A catalogue record for this book is available from the British Library

Library of Congress Cataloging-in-Publication Data
A catalog record for this book has been requested

ISBN: 978-1-138-05113-3 (hbk)
ISBN: 978-1-03-217884-4 (pbk)
DOI: 10.4324/9781315168401

Typeset in Times New Roman
by Apex CoVantage, LLC

Contents

Figures

Acknowledgements

This book and the research and design artefacts underpinning it would not have been possible without the support, guidance and help of others.

First, to Stephen Viller and John Harrison, who supervised the PhD thesis that formed the basis of this book: I am grateful to you both for your sage advice and ongoing encouragement over several years. Thanks also to the thesis examiners, who provided critical and valuable feedback.

The prototypes described here were made possible thanks to the study participants and later with the creative and technical abilities of Andrea Epifani and David Lloyd, who invested many hours developing the NewsCube beta version. The creation of that tool, and subsequent release of open source code, was made possible by a Walkley Grant for Innovation in Journalism. Thanks to the team at the Walkley Foundation for their support, and to the team at iLab, who gave valuable guidance on pitching for the money. Thanks also to the Journalism Design students whose projects are discussed here.

I must thank Bob Franklin and the editorial team at Routledge for their support of the book proposal and its subsequent production. Also thanks to the anonymous reviewers for their feedback. The draft manuscript was read critically by colleagues at the University of Queensland: Jane Johnston and Tom O'Regan. Thank you both for your time and insights; the book is better for your input.

I must also acknowledge the ongoing support and friendship of the members of the University of Queensland's interaction design research group.

Finally, thanks to Mark and Gabriel, who have supported my work over many years and never tired of listening to me talk about it.

Thank you everyone.

Abbreviations

HCI	human-computer interaction
IoT	internet of things
IxD	interaction design
JxD	Journalism Design
QR code	quick response code
RtD	Research through Design
ubicomp	ubiquitous computing
VSD	Value Sensitive Design

1   Journalism Design

Journalism Design is about the future – not predicting the future, but imagining and creating it. It is about what journalism might become as technologies increasingly, and continually, reshape the way we interact with information, with each other and with our environment. It is about how journalists can regain some control over their practice and draw on their expertise to determine how technology, and the changes it brings, will reshape their future. Journalism Design is about building journalistic resilience.

News organisations find themselves in a struggle for survival. In this situation, future thinking is essential. Although multimedia, social media and algorithmic media have moved into newsrooms and forced some changes to journalistic practice, for the most part this has been a process of adaptation rather than innovation: social platforms and digital tools have been developed by technology companies and taken up by journalists as their audiences have migrated to what has been called 'the platform press' (Bell and Owen 2017). New technologies have been imposed upon newsrooms, and journalists have had to adjust their practices to them.

The impact this has had on news organisations is profound. Not only are Facebook, Google and Apple now dominant news publishers, but the financial strength of these companies means they are also leaders in research and development and are in position to acquire other companies to complement their existing services (Moore 2016). As a result, news companies are increasingly being left out of an equation in which technology companies control the hardware, software and networks on which their audiences communicate. As Pavlik and Bridges (2013) point out, this is an equation in which the news media once had a central position. Where newspapers, radio and television were once platforms in their own right – controlling the creation, distribution and monetisation of their content – these providers now help fill the platforms of others. The disruption has prompted calls for a redistribution of wealth from technology companies to media companies (Bell 2017), for new journalistic practice (Picard 2009), and for news organisations to innovate and find ways to offer new value to audiences (Christensen et al. 2012).

Journalism has long relied on notions of social responsibility, truth and independence to justify its value to society and to democracy more broadly. Spikes in subscriptions to publications such as *The New York Times* in the wake of Donald Trump's election in 2016 suggest readers value this traditional journalistic role. But the story is patchy: soon after reports of increased sales of quality papers in the United States, there was yet another round of job cuts in Australian newsrooms. What journalists and audiences see as valuable is not necessarily the same. As Picard (2010) points out, the notion that the underlying social and democratic value of journalism is 'good' does not necessarily translate to value for audiences who seek functional, emotional and self-expressive benefit from news.

New platforms and interfaces could enable journalism to deliver these values and others to readers. Wearable computing, ambient environments and tangible interfaces are just some of the emerging technologies that promise us new and different ways of interacting with information, with each other and with the world. But this will have implications for the way journalists *do* journalism and *what* is considered journalism.

Imagine a future where journalism is less about news and more about provoking experiences that make citizens think about issues from multiple perspectives, or where journalists build public interfaces for informing communities about how they are responding to issues such as reducing emissions or tackling chronic health issues. Scenarios such as these are certainly feasible from a technology perspective, but they suggest changes in practice and thinking on the part of the journalist. For instance, news stories may not be necessary, and the traditionally independent journalist might need to take a position on an issue in order to engage the public. There are also the problems of technical capability and how to pay for infrastructure that serves the public interest.

Journalists, and much of their audience, often see technology as something that improves what they are doing or that makes it more convenient: social media pushes stories to more places; mobile notifications provide immediacy on the move; and artificial intelligence releases journalists from some of the more mundane reporting tasks. There is a view that 'technology changes, journalism doesn't' (Marconi et al. 2017, p. 19). But it is entirely possible that the media of the future will not resemble, or require, any of the formats or structures that journalists are familiar with. The pace of technological change means we can't really predict what technologies we will be using in ten years' time or who will invent or control them.

This book argues that rather than adapting journalism to new technologies, journalists should be creating the technologies themselves. Rather than pushing stories to social and mobile platforms, journalists should take a role in inventing the platforms and devices. Instead of optimising journalism for technology, journalists should consider how to design the technology for journalism and redesign the journalism that is produced. And they should put core values of journalism – rather than production processes, story formats or social metrics – at the fore. This might mean a renewed focus on communities, and it might mean journalism is practiced in design studios and technology companies as well as media organisations.

This is not a radical idea – Pavlik (2013) has argued that innovation in journalism should be guided by core principles – but it is a provocative idea. It calls for a proactive view of technology and a willingness to challenge established practice. It could mean a more active role on the part of the journalist: active in the issues concerning publics, and in the development of the technologies that address those issues. Designing technologies means redesigning practices, and this is how we can imagine the future. The way to do this is through design.

Design refers broadly to the creative, iterative practices of designers who use sketching, making and observing to generate ideas for addressing complex problems. Design can be exploratory, social, provocative or critical, and in the case of interaction design it is concerned with technological futures. Interaction design is about imagining what might be possible or desirable with a technology and creating things that give shape and form to those possibilities. These design artefacts represent a possible future. By putting them into the world – deploying them to people who might use them – designers learn what needs to change in the present to make that future possible and how the present changes how we imagine the future.

Think about how the production and distribution of information might change if it were delivered via a coffee pot or embedded in the architecture of public buildings, or how we might develop tangible platforms for understanding social policy. Interaction design can investigate these possibilities from both the technological and the human perspectives. Through interaction design we can generate ideas for using technology for specific contexts: for particular situations, for particular people, for particular reasons. This means we can design for specific values. So, in journalism, which is underpinned by strong notions of social responsibility and the public interest, interaction design is a way to develop technologies that embody the essence of those values.

In this way, Journalism Design is about the technological possibilities for journalism as well as the journalistic possibilities for technology. Design is a way of finding out how stories and experiences might be designed for interaction as well as information, designed for values such as immersion, tactility or location, as well as the public interest. But it is also about the reverse. Through design we can infuse values such as balance, the right to know, social responsibility and editorial judgement into the design of technology. This is more of a lateral shift than an upending of the current system (Yelavich and Adams 2014), but it is a shift that suggests journalists have something meaningful to contribute, both to the future of journalism and to the future of communication technologies.

As a form of practice-led research, design tells us that knowledge can be produced through action. This is because the process of designing is reflective: as designers work, they draw on their own knowledge as well as their understanding of the context in which they are working and reflect in action (Schön 1991) on the situation and their response to it. The result is an artefact, a thing, that did not previously exist. There is something in the practice of designing, and in the judgements of the designer, that leads to new ideas. But domain knowledge also plays a role.

The technology theorist W. Brian Arthur uses the term *deep craft* to describe the expertise he sees as an important driver of innovation. He suggests that advanced, innovative technologies stem from a 'context of knowings' that provide an understanding of 'how to manipulate newly discovered or poorly understood phenomena' (Arthur 2007, p. 285). This is about translating ideas between domains, or industries, a process Arthur refers to as *redomaining*. Through a deep understanding of context and practice, it is possible for industries not only to adopt new ideas but to draw from them, combine some parts with existing parts and create something new. Deep craft provides the insight for how to do this, but '[a]s this happens, the domain of course adapts too' (Arthur 2011, p. 155).

Journalists have this deep craft. Their practice is underpinned by normative values and core tenets that give meaning and purpose to what they do. The challenge is to translate those practices to new formats, processes and experiences – shapes that may be quite different from those created before the disruption. I do not presume that the new ideas will be as financially lucrative as what came before, but as society increasingly grapples with the realities of inequality, climate change, extremism and any number of other issues that our established systems seem unable to address, stasis is not an option, and the future of journalism will almost certainly not be like its past.

This is not to say that journalism is not adapting to new conditions. Journalists and newsrooms are adopting new formats, integrating technologies and experimenting with business models. My intention is not to diminish the significance of these trends but to point out that this is reactive rather than proactive and that adapting existing processes and outputs to new platforms is not the same as inventing the platforms in the first place. Journalism Design is a way to create technologies with journalistic intention.

This book is an investigation into this idea. It draws on theory and practice to explain how journalism and design can be used together to imagine something new. This has implications for both practice and research because it is through the practice-led, experimental and reflective approach of design that journalistic futures can be imagined.

The following chapters set the theoretical and methodological context for Journalism Design. They examine technological promise and the value of design-led research. Chapter 2 considers emerging opportunities and argues that new technologies may require radically different forms of interaction. To exploit these, journalists will need to become proactive in their approach to technology and its use in their practice. The chapter examines the intersection of journalism and technology and suggests journalists could be at the centre of the design process for socially responsible tech.

Chapter 3 discusses design as a practice and as a method of research, in particular the role that design artefacts play in producing knowledge. It draws parallels between journalism and design, suggesting that design provides opportunities for innovation in both journalism practice and research.

Chapter 4 is a case study in Journalism Design. It details the design, development and evaluation of the NewsCube, a three-dimensional storytelling tool. Drawing on design activities and user feedback, it discusses how the artefact probed journalistic practice and revealed how that practice might need to change for users to take advantage of the playful, tactile interactions afforded by the NewsCube. This case reveals the importance of journalistic thinking in the design of the new concept.

Chapter 5 considers the future. It examines the work of Journalism Design students tasked with designing and prototyping journalistic interactions. Their work suggests journalism's future could be distributed among communities, studios and tech companies. The chapter ends by posing questions for further research.

I should note that I come to this research as a former journalist. I spent 12 years in reporting and production roles in newspapers and online publications in three countries before moving to academic work and doctoral study. The later years of my newsroom experience coincided with Web 2.0, and I was involved in working out how best to use digital tools to tell news stories. The possibilities were exciting, yet I observed that the needs of the newspaper were privileged over those of the Web. I came to think that journalists needed to rethink fundamentally how they could use the emerging technologies to tell stories and engage readers. Those experiences motivated my interest in academic research.

I see this book as a beginning. Its ideas are an invitation for further exploration and for deeper discussion.

References

Arthur, W.B., 2007. The structure of invention. *Research Policy*, 36 (2), 274–287.

Arthur, W.B., 2011. *The nature of technology: What it is and how it evolves*. New York: Free Press.

Bell, E., 2017. Facebook and the press: The transfer of power [online]. *Columbia Journalism Review*. Available from: www.cjr.org/tow_center/facebook-and-the-press-the-transfer-of-power.php [Accessed 30 Jul 2017].

Bell, E., and Owen, T., 2017. *The platform press: How Silicon Valley reengineered journalism*. New York: Tow Center for Digital Journalism.

Christensen, C.M., Skok, D., and Allworth, J., 2012. Breaking news: Mastering the art of disruptive innovation in journalism. *Nieman Reports*, 66 (3), 6–20.

Marconi, F., Siegman, A., and Journalist, M., 2017. *The future of augmented journalism: A guide for newsrooms in the age of smart machines*. New York: The Associated Press.

Moore, M., 2016. *Tech giants and civic power*. London: Centre for the Study of Media Communication and Power, Policy Institute, King's College London.

Pavlik, J.V., 2013. Innovation and the future of journalism. *Digital Journalism*, 1 (2), 181–193.

Pavlik, J.V., and Bridges, F., 2013. The emergence of Augmented Reality (AR) as a storytelling medium in journalism. *Journalism & Communication Monographs*, 15 (1), 4–59.

Picard, R.G., 2009. *Why journalists deserve low pay*. Presented at the Reuters Institute for the Study of Journalism seminar series, University of Oxford.

Picard, R.G., 2010. *Value creation and the future of news organisations*. Barcelona: Formalpress.

Schön, D.A., 1991. *The reflective practitioner: How professionals think in action*. 2nd ed. Farnham, England: Ashgate.

Yelavich, S., and Adams, B., eds., 2014. *Design as future-making*. London: Bloomsbury.

2 Proximate futures

In the future, robots will take our jobs, cars will fly, and everyday objects will become computers. In the future, technology will be so interwoven in our lives that we will not even notice it. Advances in machine intelligence, faster computing and smaller devices will change the way we live, work and interact with each other, and with machines. This, at least, is the promise. But just like the paperless office, reality is often quite different, and technological promise does not always translate into real life, which brings with it people, culture, laws and regulations, among other things, that impact on the way that technology is used.

Take the concept of ubiquitous computing, or ubicomp, for instance. This is the idea that computation can be transferred from desktop computers into the environment. The idea emerged late last century and has evolved to encompass concepts such as the internet of things, wearable computing, augmented reality, calm computing, pervasive computing, locative media and near-field communication, among others. Indeed, the field has become so pervasive that some have suggested it is time it disappeared (Abowd 2012).

The main drivers behind these ideas are a massive increase in computational power and an expanding context in which that power is used. In 1965, Moore's Law predicted the continued, exponential growth of computational power: that the density of components on computer chips would double every two years. This has not only proven to be the case, but similar rates have been observed in chip speeds, computer speeds and the rate of computations per unit of energy, suggesting that computing systems can maintain exponential growth (Denning and Lewis 2016).

Not only are our computers faster and more powerful, but we are seeing this power deployed in an ever-increasing number of things: cars, watches, fabric and medical devices, for instance. Computation is becoming more present in our lives and in our environment, and at times the boundary between the real and virtual is becoming porous. Virtual, augmented and mixed realities highlight the way we can intentionally meld the physical and digital worlds. The way our physical activity is automatically logged via our phone and arm band, or how search engines learn our preferences and tailor the information we retrieve is a similar blurring of this boundary. Technologies such as these are ubiquitous and almost seamlessly integrate into our everyday lives.

Yet the promises of new technologies do not always manifest, or, if they do, they often do so in ways not intended. The original promise of ubicomp, for instance, was for a seamless system of interconnected processors that would 'weave themselves into the fabric of everyday life until they are indistinguishable from it' (Weiser 1991, p. 94) and where powerful informatics never reach the surface of our awareness (Greenfield 2010). Clearly this has not yet materialised, and, while much writing on ubicomp describes a proximate future – 'one just around the corner' (Dourish and Bell 2011, p. 23) – the reality is that we have a messy, patchy network made up of inconsistent infrastructure, restricted power, and various legal, regulatory and social influences. Dourish and Bell suggest the 'practice of any technology in the world is never quite as simple, straightforward, or idealized as it is imagined to be' (p. 4).

One technology where reality is different from promise, particularly in a journalistic context, is hypertext. I have studied the journalistic application of hypertext in some depth (Doherty 2013), and the NewsCube case study, discussed later in this book, has its origins in that work. It is worth discussing here briefly, as it is a good illustration of how the promise of a technology can be different from its reality.

Linked up

Hypertext is the underlying structure of the World Wide Web and is a defining characteristic of the internet. It enables writers and publishers to create relationships between different pieces of content and to give readers a different type of control over their reading experience, such as leaving the core narrative to explore other things and returning. Indeed, there is a view that hypertext can facilitate greater depth in storytelling and allow stories to be told from multiple perspectives. There is also a view that it can deepen authors' relationships with their audiences, so it has the potential to attract new readers or keep existing ones engaged for longer.

Many of these ideas emerged among computer scientists and literary scholars. The term 'hypertext' was coined by Nelson (1965) to describe the idea that information could be connected in a non-linear way. In the three decades following, researchers explored the potential for hypertext to remedy print and enable storytelling from multiple perspectives, and they examined how shape and space might be used to help readers navigate and comprehend hypertext narratives. This work resulted in authoring systems and hypertext literature: *Afternoon, a Story* (Joyce 1987), *Patchwork Girl* (Jackson 1995) and *Victory Garden* (Moulthrop 1995) are well-known examples in which the reader decides the order of events. In the case of *Patchwork Girl*, readers build a visual representation of the main character as they read snippets about various parts of her body. The narrative emerges through her limbs, head, features and torso, and the reader can construct the story in any order. Stories such as this do not follow a traditional plot structure or narrative arc. Instead, the readers are active participants; they have a level of control over their experience. But because hyperspace is boundless, unconstrained by time, as in a film, or space like a book, comprehension can become a problem, and readers can become lost in a story or lost to other parts of the internet. As a result, navigation becomes vital, and visualisation and shape become valuable strategies for reader comprehension, hence the building of a body.

In journalism, hypertext is most obvious in the links that pepper individual online stories or as a tool to package long-running coverage of a topic. Hypertext is seen as a way to give stories greater interactivity, credibility, transparency and diversity (De Maeyer 2012), and stories by publishers such as ProPublica in the United States and SBS in Australia have shown how hypertext can be used to allow a reader to explore source materials or navigate a virtual representation of a real environment. The examples I am thinking of here are parts of ProPublica's 'Post Mortem' investigation (Allan 2011), which allowed readers to enter a database separate from the story and read primary documents and notes. The other is *The Block* (Smith 2012), which allowed readers to move through a virtual neighbourhood, meeting characters in the places where they lived and worked. Readers could then watch recorded interviews or read archival material.

However, such examples are exceptions, and generally journalists favour linear text and prefer to use links to create relationships between stories on the same website rather than linking to primary sources or related background information (see studies by Tsui 2008; Larrondo Ureta 2011). Similarly, from a research perspective, journalism scholars have neglected more advanced hypertext concepts such as navigating virtual, boundless space, or the ability to alter story plot. Instead, there is a tendency to study journalistic hypertext from a content perspective using content analysis techniques to examine the number and destination of links in stories. There is little experimentation with tools and the result is that we understand what is rather than what could be.

Yet in some ways early hypertext theories of distributed information, reader involvement and multiple perspectives are manifest in contemporary social networks. Platforms such as Facebook and Twitter enable readers to create networks of information and people. The enthusiastic involvement of journalists and news organisations on these platforms means that information and, by extension, narrative are distributed across a network and that users can link news stories to personal status updates and comments, thereby creating their own narratives and their own networks. It seems hyperlinks have found a calling and readers have gained some power, just not in the way imagined by hypertext theorists. And, in the case of journalism, what can be achieved in fiction does not often translate to news.

The ability of these social hypertexts to engage audiences and provide new sources of information has, in turn, impacted the way journalists go about their work. Social networks are used to source and verify stories, and news is distributed and amplified via these networks alongside more traditional media. Hermida (2010) points out that these platforms blur the boundaries between newsmakers, reporters and consumers; and Sheller (2015) suggests that not only has the imagined wall between news producers and consumers broken down, to the point where both co-produce and share content, but news events and news of events are also now mixed together in the dynamic news cycle. This blurring of the boundary between news production and consumption has been driven by technology. However, there is a human element also, and events such as the 2011 Arab Spring and the more recent US presidential election illustrate how the experience of using new platforms not only encourages new practice but can prompt reflection on core aspects of established practice.

In the Middle East, Twitter served as a common medium for both professional and citizen journalists, who together constituted 'a particular kind of online press' (Lotan et al. 2011, p. 1400). The #Egypt hashtag was constructed collaboratively by citizens, bloggers, activists, journalists and media outlets, resulting in news feeds that blended opinion, fact and emotion – 'compelling and engaging for readers, but not necessarily compatible with fact checking processes of western paradigms of journalism' (Papacharissi and de Fatima Oliveira 2012, p. 279). Similarly, during the 2016 American presidential election, false news stories about the candidates produced by teenagers in Romania were circulating on social networks alongside reports by professional journalists. Such stories have been blamed for influencing the outcome of the election, and, although academic studies are yet to verify this, Allcott and Gentzkow (2017) point out the spread of false information has both private and social costs. They say fake news is motivated by money or ideology and that while some consumers may enjoy partisan stories, fake news makes it 'more difficult for consumers to infer the true state of the world' (p. 232), and this has implications for democratic society more broadly.

The ability for networked technologies to diversify news has enriched and expanded journalism practice, but it also prompts important questions about the journalist's role in society. Certainly, the election of Donald Trump has prompted soul searching on the part of both news organisations and social networks, with Facebook promising action by deploying a combination of artificial intelligence and people.

Things to come

We are told algorithms can be put to work collecting and analysing facts, and, indeed, one vision of the future envisages machines taking over some of the more mundane aspects of journalistic work, making reporting more convenient, enabling the journalist to multitask and produce an investigative story in minutes (Marconi and Siegman 2017). Using robots to sort truth from fiction and to speed up the reporting process are convenient applications of machine intelligence in journalism. However, beneath the surface, emerging insights into algorithmic journalism tell us that the junction of people and computation is less about collaboration and more about using computers to replicate established journalistic practices. In this case, technology promises to automate the news-production process and produce high volumes of content at minimal cost.

We are beginning to see regular studies of the potential for and perceptions of software-generated news. It seems that audiences are happy to read a robot report and, in fact, see very little difference between those and stories written by journalists (Clerwall 2014). Indeed, journalists themselves seem content to work alongside the robots, seeing automated content as freeing them up to work on more 'human' tasks such as creativity, analysis and personality (Dalen 2012). But this could have two outcomes: journalists could become redundant, or competition could force the humans 'to become even better at those tasks where they can make a difference' (p. 653).

Yet there is another issue here: that of engrained journalistic practice. As Young and Hermida (2015) point out, the programs creating automated news are themselves an expression of basic journalistic norms and practices. In studying the *Los Angeles Times*' 'The Homicide Report' website, they found that despite the use of algorithms, journalists 'returned to familiar, historic, and gendered practices' to supply the emotional and human-interest context, and that while robo-posts 'extend professional expertise in journalism to include the identities of the programmer and non-human actor, [they] are themselves an expression of basic norms and practices with respect to reporting homicide, albeit with greater completeness' (p. 393).

This highlights an important aspect of journalism in relation to new technologies: that established practice can inhibit the ability for the profession to extend and expand concepts around interaction in these new settings. Like the hyperlinks in standard news stories, robot-generated reports are not challenging established journalistic forms. Perhaps this is simply the result of technologies that can be easily adapted to existing practice: hyperlinks fit neatly into inverted pyramids – stories that organise information in order of perceived importance – and that story shape can be easily programmed. But what happens when technology demands entirely different styles of content delivery and audience interaction? The technology literature tells us that the future of computing will allow us to interact with people, objects and information in physical or digital form, using touch, sound or biometric interfaces. Our interactions with media could become even more fragmented, across platforms, objects and environments. Virtual realities could become blended with real life. In this future, traditional journalistic outputs, like news stories, may not be fit for the types of interaction demanded by new technologies.

Pavlik and Bridges (2013) see potential for virtual reality to 'create a form of storytelling that is more about citizen engagement in a participatory, first-person narrative form' (p. 51). Similarly, the internet of things (IoT) promises content and services will be all around us and always available, 'paving the way to new applications, enabling new ways of working; new ways of interacting; new ways of entertainment; new ways of living' (Miorandi et al. 2012, p. 1497). It sounds transformative, and certainly if objects themselves begin interacting socially with each other to build communication networks, as Atzori et al. (2014) expect, then journalists will need to consider how best to engage with both connected things and people.

Urban informatics offers interesting possibilities too. Those studying smart cities see potential for urban environments to foster public participation and governance. Foth et al. (2015) envision cities in which 'touch points' between the architecture and the citizens encourage some of the public participation in Dutton's (2009) idea of the Fifth Estate. The Fifth Estate is based on the idea that networked individuals can themselves 'enable a new source of accountability in government, politics and other sectors' (p. 1).

It is distinct from the legislative, executive, judicial branches of government, as well as the media. The challenge for journalists is to understand how they fit into such an environment and how the products they make – today it is news, but, in the future, it may be something else – might be consumed or used in these contexts.

While technologies offer opportunities for new and radically different forms of interaction, we also know that established practices, uncertainty about the future, and the priorities of social platforms constrain the ability for news organisations to fully explore and exploit these opportunities.

Risk for uncertain reward

Research into how news organisations have coped with new technologies tell two stories: one of stasis and one of risk. In the early years of the internet, ethnographic studies of newsrooms (for instance, Boczkowski 2005; Domingo 2008) found that journalists and editors tended to simply adopt new platforms, without altering their underlying attitudes and practices. Journalists seemed to prefer linear text over hypertext and multimedia, and traditional norms of gatekeeping over participatory journalism and alternative flows of information (Steensen 2011). There was a view that journalistic attitudes and established practices hampered the ability of news organisations to adapt, with Ryfe (2012) arguing that the challenge was ontological, not technological or economic: journalists were invested in prior successes and 'constitutive rules' that structure their interactions and 'anchors journalism to tradition' (p. 116).

The emergence of social and mobile media, apps and start-up culture has brought change. There is a 'more aggressive and enterprising approach to digital media' (Kalogeropoulos and Nielsen 2017), a willingness to work alongside robots (Marconi et al. 2017) and the emergence of tech-focused, digital-only publishers where flatter structures and collaborative work encourage innovation, creativity and risk (Boyles 2016). But all the while, journalists are in a state of uncertainty: on the one hand tailoring and tweaking content for optimisation on social platforms, on the other increasingly worried about growing dependence on these intermediaries (Kleis Nielsen and Ganter 2017). A key tension is a lack of transparency about how platforms privilege content and the risk that the rules might change. Where once news values determined the worth of journalistic content, now it could be reach, genre or length of video, and, as Bell and Owen (2017) point out, '[t]his inevitably changes the presentation and tone of the journalism itself' (p. 39).

The ability for journalists to make judgements about news based on social and democratic values is fundamental to the legitimacy of journalistic practice, so the erosion of that function in favour of the priorities of social platforms is cause for concern. Some have suggested those core values need to change. Steel (2017) suggests that the ability for journalism 'to reflect and represent the interests of the public has long been open to question' (p. 37) and suggests that uncritical acceptance of cherished norms and core values means journalism now requires fundamental reconsideration. Similarly, Josephi (2013) suggests that promotion of core values has forestalled any radical reorganisation of journalism in the face of economic pressures, and Hujanen (2016) questions whether participatory communication means core journalistic values need to change.

I am not convinced that core values are the core problem. Rather, it is the way those values are realised – through news production processes, through journalistic outputs and in the culture surrounding that work – that has stymied new ideas. This has been compounded by the fact that news organisations are following, not leading, technological advancement.

Although journalists have appropriated social platforms, added links to stories and accepted robots to the editorial team, in most cases they have not constructed these technologies and do not control them. Moreover, the technology companies that own the platforms also own the information about audiences and so can monetise the content of others. This creates tension, both economically and socially. By distributing but not creating content, social platforms have not only profited from journalistic labour, but, because audiences have moved as well, so too have advertising revenues, and so the financial return to journalism is diminished. At the same time, journalists' commitment to core values and social responsibilities means they are bound to standards of professional practice that companies such as Facebook are not. Yet in an environment where user-generated content is distributed and amplified alongside journalism, where good reporting is not algorithmically privileged by social networks (Bell and Owen 2017), and where 'fake news' can be as influential as the press in democratic society, then journalistic values seem vital.

This does not mean that journalists, or news organisations, are vital.

Tech and values

It is possible to develop new platforms and interactions around values – to let what is important to people be the impetus behind new technological development rather than the promise of a technology itself. Among design researchers there is a recognition that as technologies become more pervasive and intelligent, they will need to embody a sense of humanity. Moore points out the heads of big Silicon Valley companies 'frequently talk about their mission to be a force for good in the world and to change the world for the better' (Moore 2016, p. 20). We also see this idea playing out in discussion around ethics in artificial intelligence (Bostrom and Yudkowsky 2014) and in the hopes for smart urban environments.

In the case of designing cities for public participation, Foth and co-authors (2015) argue that although social media can foster civic engagement, the sophisticated filters and recommendation systems of networks such as Facebook and Google do not necessarily serve the public interest: 'With the absence of a journalistic or editorial code of ethics, these algorithms [. . .] are optimised to prioritise content that will generate more traffic' (p. 626). The tendency for commercial platforms to cater to individual preferences means these platforms 'will not bring about a quantum change in the practice and impact of civic engagement' (p. 626).

There is an opportunity for principles of research, freedom of speech, trust and ethics to underpin journalistic innovation (Pavlik 2013) and inform the design of new technologies. However, journalists are not the only ones in position to provide an appropriate value system. There is an emerging consensus that design is a value-laden activity, that the outcomes of design work incorporate values, and that practitioners should explicitly address values (JafariNaimi et al. 2015). In the field of human-computer interaction (HCI), there is a growing recognition that computing needs to embody human values (Harper et al. 2008), and Dourish and Bell (2011) have called for a deeper understanding of society and culture in relation to emerging technologies, because '[i]t is lived and embodied practice [. . .] that gives form and meaning to technology' (p. 73). Tonkinwise (2017) calls on designers to play a role in helping society better understand the Anthropocene and to 'take responsibility for designing our way toward preferred futures' (n.p.). Certainly, designers have developed various approaches that focus on designing for values, and some of these aim to achieve the goals that have traditionally occupied journalists.

Value Sensitive Design (VSD), for instance, highlights trust, accountability, freedom from bias, access, autonomy, privacy and consent, although Friedman et al. (2013) define values as anything a person or group considers important in life. Their approach demands extensive investigation to understand what is important to people before design begins, but it seeks to influence the design of technology so that it 'accounts for human values in a principled and comprehensive manner' (p. 55). JafariNaimi and co-authors (2015) point out that the logic of identifying and then applying values suggests they are something that can be addressed separately from action, whereas, in reality, designers make sense of values through the process of designing: values are intertwined with practice. They also point out that not all values are valuable.

By contrast, social design is about creating artefacts or systems that empower people to take collective action regarding issues that concern them. The approach has roots in participatory design and social innovation, and it weaves social activity with the creation of things and services to create value (Chen et al. 2016). Social design projects often take place in public spaces, communities and grassroots organisations, and the design process focuses on imagining alternative futures. Le Dantec (2016) points out that in social design, emphasis is placed on bringing people together to address issues 'rather than on how to use design to further segment and isolate individuals for targeted consumption' (p. 26).

The way journalists deal with values sits somewhere between these two approaches: like VSD, notions of trust, balance, ethics and social responsibility exist prior to reporting, but they are negotiated in the context of specific stories through journalistic action. Conversely, the idea of independence to some extent precludes journalism from engaging in the interventions of social design, although some think journalists should become more vested in the people and issues they report (Ryfe 2012). What differentiates journalism here is that journalistic values are tacit; they are part of a journalist's engrained knowledge and practice. The journalistic process does not reveal values as much as it reinforces what journalism is, so, while designers could no doubt create new and engaging news experiences, it is journalists who have the deep craft (Arthur 2007).

However, the idea of designing for values does present the possibility of designing for journalistic values and suggests an important role for the engrained, tacit knowledge in journalistic practice, perhaps just not in the way some journalists imagine. There is potential for journalists to play a meaningful role in the design of cities, robots, internet-connected things and alternative realities, but this will require journalists to envision a role outside the newsroom and beyond the production of news. This will mean seeing themselves as part of a digitally connected community, and they will need to understand how to use technologies, along with journalistic values, to work in the public interest. In short, they will need to be proactive, and this brings us back to ubicomp.

Proactive journalists

The disconnect between the promise and reality of ubicomp has prompted debate about the role of people as technology becomes more powerful. Rogers (2006, 2009) points out that technologies are changing the way we live. Not only are we increasingly dependent on software and hardware to help us to communicate and manage our lives, but we allow computers to act on our behalf, to decide the route to a destination, to remind us of appointments and events. In response, Rogers advocates for a shift away from the idea of proactive computing – computers programmed to take the initiative on behalf of people – to proactive people, where ubicomp technologies are designed to engage people more actively in what they already do. Computing, in her view, should be enabling and should 'provoke us to learn, understand and reflect

more upon our interactions with technologies and each other'
(2006, p. 412). She argues that 'we need to design new technologies to encourage people to be proactive in their lives, performing
ever greater feats, extending their ability to learn, make decisions,
reason, create, solve complex problems and generate innovative
ideas' (2009, p. 10).

Applied to journalism, this view would put journalists at the
centre of the design process for public interest technology. Rather
than simply adopting technologies, journalists would create software, devices and interactions to achieve journalistic goals and
embody journalistic values. To do this, journalists would need to
draw on their deep knowledge of their craft and combine that with
new approaches to practice and research.

Established forms of journalistic practice alone are not condu-
cive to this change. Ethnographers have noted the reluctance of
working journalists to break with entrenched modes of production.
But another challenge is the gulf that exists between journalism
practice and journalism research – often the concerns of journalism academics are not the same as those of journalism practitioners. Several scholars have observed methodological challenges in
journalism research, which is dominated by content analysis, surveys and interviews. Unlike the computer scientists and literary
scholars who created authoring systems and experimented with
narrative as a way of exploring hypertext, journalism researchers
tended to study hypertext retrospectively by counting links and
exploring where they went. Focusing on destination, discourse
or frames told researchers much about how hypertext was used
but did not allow them to explore how space, shape or navigation
might push stories beyond a digital inverted pyramid. A different
approach may have led to different questions and outcomes, perhaps with implications for future practice.

This idea is at the heart of this book. To imagine possible futures,
to understand how journalism might inform the development of
technology, we need a way of experimenting with and evaluating journalism in new contexts. This is about designing technologies that extend and change journalism. The social designers tell
us that it is possible to shape ideas around what is important to
people and communities. This means we could design for what
is distinctive about journalism and valuable to audiences. But

technological possibility is also a factor, and to understand the junction of people and tech, we need to look to another facet of design: interaction. Interaction design is concerned with the inter-section of people and technology and it seeks to create ideas for using technologies in daily life. By designing for people and their lived experience, this approach can be applied to many aspects of journalism. It means that new ideas can be imagined and pro-totyped and that journalists can begin to understand the implica-tions new ideas have for their practice and how their practice can inform new technologies.

References

Abowd, G.D., 2012. What next, ubicomp? celebrating an intellectual disappear-ing act. In: A.K. Dey, H-H. Chu, and G. Hayes, eds. *Proceedings of the 2012 ACM conference on ubiquitous computing*. New York: ACM Press, 31–40.

Allan, M., 2011. Why can't Linda Carswell get her husband's heart back? [online]. ProPublica. Available from: www.propublica.org/article/why-cant-linda-carswell-get-her-husbands-heart-back [Accessed 7 Jun 2017].

Allcott, H., and Gentzkow, M., 2017. Social media and fake news in the 2016 election. *Journal of Economic Perspectives*, 31 (2), 211–236.

Arthur, W.B., 2007. The structure of invention. *Research Policy*, 36 (2), 274–287.

Atzori, L., Iera, A., and Morabito, G., 2014. From 'smart objects' to 'social objects': The next evolutionary step of the internet of things. *IEEE Com-munications Magazine*, 52 (1), 97–105.

Bell, E., and Owen, T., 2017. *The platform press: How Silicon Valley reengi-neered journalism*. New York: Tow Center for Digital Journalism.

Boczkowski, P.J., 2005. *Digitizing the news: Innovation in online newspa-pers*. Cambridge, MA: MIT Press.

Bostrom, N., and Yudkowsky, E., 2014. The ethics of artificial intelligence. In: K. Frankish and W.M. Ramsey, eds. *The Cambridge handbook of artifi-cial intelligence*. Cambridge: Cambridge University Press, 316–333.

Boyles, J.L., 2016. The isolation of innovation: Restructuring the digital newsroom through intrapreneurship. *Digital Journalism*, 4 (2), 229–246.

Chen, D-S., Lu-Lin, C., Hummels, C., and Koskinen, I., 2016. Social design: An introduction. *International Journal of Design*, 10 (1).

Clerwall, C., 2014. Enter the robot journalist: Users' perceptions of auto-mated content. *Journalism Practice*, 8 (5), 519–531.

Dalen, A. van, 2012. The algorithms behind the headlines: How machine-written news redefines the core skills of human journalists. *Journalism Practice*, 6 (5–6), 648–658.

De Maeyer, J., 2012. The journalistic hyperlink: Prescriptive discourses about linking in online news. *Journalism Practice*, 6 (5–6), 692–701.

Denning, P.J., and Lewis, T.G., 2016. Exponential laws of computing growth. *Communication of the ACM*, 60 (1), 54–65.

Doherty, S., 2013. Hypertext and journalism: Paths for future research. *Digital Journalism*, 2 (2), 124–139.

Domingo, D., 2008. Interactivity in the daily routines of online newsrooms: Dealing with an uncomfortable myth. *Journal of Computer-Mediated Communication*, 13 (3), 680–704.

Dourish, P., and Bell, G., 2011. *Diving a digital future: Mess and mythology in ubiquitous computing*. 1st ed. Cambridge, MA: MIT Press.

Dutton, W.H., 2009. The Fifth Estate emerging through the network of networks. *Prometheus*, 27 (1), 1–15.

Foth, M., Tomitsch, M., Satchell, C., and Haeusler, M.H., 2015. *From users to citizens: Some thoughts on designing for polity and civics*. New York: ACM Press, 623–633.

Friedman, B., Kahn, P.H., and Borning, A., 2013. Value sensitive design and information systems. In: N. Doorn, D. Schuurbiers, I. van de Poel, and M.E. Gorman, eds. *Early engagement and new technologies: Opening up the laboratory*. Dordrecht: Springer Netherlands, 55–95.

Greenfield, A., 2010. *Everyware: The dawning age of ubiquitous computing*. Berkeley, CA: New Riders.

Harper, R., Rodden, T., Rogers, Y., and Sellen, A., eds., 2008. *Being human: human-computer interaction in the year 2020*. Cambridge, England: Microsoft Research.

Hermida, A., 2010. Twittering the news: The emergence of ambient journalism. *Journalism Practice*, 4 (3), 297–308.

Hujanen, J., 2016. Participation and the blurring values of journalism. *Journalism Studies*, 17 (7), 871–880.

Jackson, S., 1995. *Patchwork girl*. Watertown, MA: Eastgate Systems.

JafariNaimi, N., Nathan, L., and Hargraves, I., 2015. Values as hypotheses: Design, inquiry, and the service of values. *Design Issues*, 31 (4), 91–104.

Josephi, B., 2013. How much democracy does journalism need? *Journalism*, 14 (4), 474–489.

Joyce, M., 1987. *Afternoon, a story*. Watertown, MA: Eastgate Systems.

Kalogeropoulos, A., and Nielsen, R.K., 2017. Investing in online video news: A cross-national analysis of news organizations' enterprising approach to digital media. *Journalism Studies*, 0 (0), 1–18.

Kleis Nielsen, R., and Ganter, S.A., 2017. Dealing with digital intermediaries: A case study of the relations between publishers and platforms. *New Media & Society*, 1461444817701318.

Larrondo Ureta, A., 2011. The potential of web-only feature stories: A case study of Spanish media sites. *Journalism Studies*, 12 (2), 188–204.

Le Dantec, C.A., 2016. Design through collective action/collective action through design. *Interactions*, 24 (1), 24–30.

Lotan, G., Graeff, E., Ananny, M., Gaffney, D., Pearce, I., and Boyd, D., 2011. The revolutions were tweeted: Information flows during the 2011 Tunisian and Egyptian revolutions. *International Journal of Communication*, 5 (0), 31.

Marconi, F., and Siegman, A., 2017. A day in the life of a journalist in 2027: Reporting meets AI. *Columbia Journalism Review*.

Marconi, F., Siegman, A., and Journalist, M., 2017. *The future of augmented journalism: A guide for newsrooms in the age of smart machines*. New York: The Associated Press.

Miorandi, D., Sicari, S., De Pellegrini, F., and Chlamtac, I., 2012. Internet of things: Vision, applications and research challenges. *Ad Hoc Networks*, 10 (7), 1497–1516.

Moore, M., 2016. *Tech giants and civic power*. London: Centre for the Study of Media Communication and Power, Policy Institute, King's College London.

Moulthrop, S., 1995. *Victory garden*. Watertown, MA: Eastgate Systems.

Nelson, T.H., 1965. Complex information processing: A file structure for the complex, the changing and the indeterminate. In: L. Winner, ed. *Proceedings of the 1965 20th national conference*. New York: ACM Press, 84–100.

Papacharissi, Z., and de Fatima Oliveira, M., 2012. Affective news and networked publics: The rhythms of news storytelling on #Egypt. *Journal of Communication*, 62 (2), 266–282.

Pavlik, J.V., 2013. Innovation and the future of journalism. *Digital Journalism*, 1 (2), 181–193.

Pavlik, J.V., and Bridges, F., 2013. The emergence of augmented reality (AR) as a storytelling medium in journalism. *Journalism & Communication Monographs*, 15 (1), 4–59.

Rogers, Y., 2006. Moving on from Weiser's vision of calm computing: Engaging ubicomp experiences. In: *International conference on ubiquitous computing*. New York: Springer, 404–421.

Rogers, Y., 2009. The changing face of human-computer interaction in the age of ubiquitous computing. In: A. Holzinger and K. Miesenberger, eds. *Symposium of the Austrian HCI and usability engineering group*. New York: Springer, 1–19.

Ryfe, D.M., 2012. *Can journalism survive: An inside look at American newsrooms*. Cambridge: Polity Press.

Sheller, M., 2015. News now: Interface, ambience, flow, and the disruptive spatio-temporalities of mobile news media. *Journalism Studies*, 16 (1), 12–26.

Smith, M., 2012. The block: Stories from a meeting place [online]. *SBS*. Available from: www.sbs.com.au/theblock [Accessed 7 Jun 2017].

Steel, J., 2017. Reappraising journalism's normative foundations. In: C. Peters and M. Broersma, eds. *Rethinking journalism again*. Abingdon: Routledge, 35–48.

Steensen, S., 2011. Online journalism and the promises of new technology: A critical review and look ahead. *Journalism Studies*, 12 (3), 311–327.

Tonkinwise, C., 2017. Design thinking, yet again, because, maybe, it could actually be useful, perhaps even necessary. . . . *Medium*.

Tsui, L., 2008. The hyperlink in newspapers and blogs. In: J. Turow and L. Tsui, eds. *Hyperlinked society: Questioning connections in the digital age*. Ann Arbor: University of Michigan Press, 70–84.

Weiser, M., 1991. The computer for the 21st century. *Scientific American*, 265 (3), 94–104.

Young, M.L., and Hermida, A., 2015. From Mr. and Mrs. Outlier to central tendencies: Computational journalism and crime reporting at the Los Angeles Times. *Digital Journalism*, 3 (3), 381–397.

3 Design, journalism and knowledge

Journalism and interaction design have a lot in common. They are both largely concerned with people, they both draw on qualitative techniques such as interview and observation to understand situations, and they are both creative, reflexive practices that produce things that are used in the world. But where journalism is rooted in the present, near past (the first draft of history no less) and prospective future, interaction design looks to imagined possibilities and ideal futures. Where the journalist imagines what might be probable or likely given a set of circumstances, the designer imagines what is desirable and considers how to bring that into being. In this way, design produces things that represent possibilities, which can challenge the present and prospective future, and this makes it valuable to both journalism practice and journalism research.

Interaction design, or IxD as it is abbreviated, 'is about creating user experiences that enhance and augment the way people work, communicate, and interact' (Rogers et al. 2011, p. 9). A tendency to focus on digital technology means it is closely aligned with human-computer interaction (HCI), and the terms are often used interchangeably. However, the fields differ. Where HCI emerged from engineering and psychology, IxD is more firmly positioned in practice-led creative design. This means that rather than the engineering design approach, which assumes problems can be solved, creative design explores the interplay between problem and possibility: 'In this interplay, the design space is explored through the creation of many parallel ideas and concepts' (Löwgren 1995, p. 88). As a result, IxD researchers take an iterative approach to addressing situations: ideas are researched, designed, prototyped, deployed to users for evaluation, and then improved, using methods such as observing, sketching and building.

This focus on making things that are useful has made design attractive to product developers and entrepreneurs, and design thinking has gained traction as a process that enables companies, individuals, start-ups and not-for-profit organisations to create products that meet the needs of their customers and clients. Indeed, there is a body of literature that links design with innovation (Brown 2008, 2009; Müller and Thoring 2012; Plattner et al. 2015) with scholars and entrepreneurs alike seeing value in designers' user-focused, creative approach as a way of addressing issues and inventing new things. As an academic discipline, design emphasises designerly practice as a means of inquiry and a way of changing situations through designed artefacts. Löwgren and Stolterman (2004) see design practices as 'tools for thought' that help to produce new knowledge. Through the process of designing, issues are investigated, possibilities are explored and new futures can be imagined. Designers themselves are part of this creative process, and the decisions and judgements they make in addressing what are often complex situations influence the outcomes of this inquiry.

Parallels can be drawn here with journalism: a practice that deals with divergent and unpredictable combinations of people, situations, facts, obfuscation and lies. To manage this, the journalist makes judgements about information and people, about how to deal with ethical or moral conflicts, and how best to serve the public interest. The stories they produce are a product of these decisions and the practices of the individual journalist – though often these decisions are guided and constrained by the priorities of news organisations and the demands of the production process. The idea that practice can be used as an approach to research also resonates with some discussions within journalism studies (Niblock 2012), although, within journalism research, it is rare to find studies that use design methods as means of inquiry. Journalism has tended to receive more attention from designers than journalism researchers have paid to interaction design. Recently, however, some collaborations between the two groups have highlighted the potential for journalists to play an active role in the development of social projects.

In Sweden, two co-design projects aimed to develop grassroots media: one, a mobile broadcaster for cultural events; the other, a week-long street-journalism experiment to raise money for humanitarian purposes. Both these projects involved a range of participants including community and commercial organisations, volunteers and design researchers. In the first project, one professional journalist was involved, and, in the second, a television station and a radio broadcaster were stakeholders. Björgvinsson (2014) explains that the projects explore decentralised media practice and 'civil political engagement conducted outside the official political system and outside and at the periphery of the established media landscape' (p. 227). By involving hip-hop artists and cultural workers in the production of video blogs and live mobile content in partnership with media organisations, the projects opened a space for both experimentation and real-life practice. The media companies gained insights about mobile video and audience interaction through designing prototypes, and the participants learned new production skills.

However, Björgvinsson points out that the goals of both groups did not always align and that the requirements of, variously, an IT company and commercial broadcasters strongly influenced the nature of the projects, so, although all those involved were willing to 'chart unknown territories and participate in new collaborations' (p. 248), it was the smaller partners – hip-hop artists, rather that media professionals – who were most willing to explore new possibilities.

In England, the Bespoke project was a collaboration between designers and non-professional journalists that aimed to develop community technologies: Viewpoint, a system to capture views of local issues; and Wayfinder, a digital signpost. This project used journalism as the interface between residents and the design team, with citizen reporters gathering information, disseminating project updates and evaluating designs. The project led to the idea of Insight Journalism (Blum-Ross et al. 2013; Taylor et al. 2014) as a way of democratising the process of designing for civic and social issues, although Taylor and co-authors note it must be understood as 'a process of building relationships and competencies' (p. 171). The focus on community was strong in Bespoke, with journalism seen as a way of helping the designers to understand the community and of holding the designers accountable for the decisions they made and the technologies they created.

These projects all focus on designing for community interests, and they suggest journalistic practices have value outside of journalism. Through experimentation with new processes and the creation of new artefacts, the projects explore new possibilities and hint at an alternative future in which journalism contributes to cultural production at a grassroots level. However, it is worth noting that in the Bespoke project, there was a view that the link between design and journalism was tenuous, with designers 'questioning the extent to which they had truly been informed by the journalism' (Taylor et al. 2014, p. 3001). This reinforces the relatively traditional approach to journalism practice that the project employed: journalists (albeit amateur reporters) collected information and were a conduit between the community and the design team; they were not integrated into the design process. Indeed, the researchers noted many of these reporters lacked the confidence and critical skills of professional journalists.

Journalism Design does not presume journalists will perform a traditional role. Journalism Design sees journalism as a creative process underpinned by a set of core values that when combined with design, enables a new form of practice. This practice draws on and may operate in concert with more traditional processes of reporting, but it is not defined by them. This alternative view of practice requires an alternative view of research – as centrally examined in this book – which requires journalism scholarship to explore what might be, rather than the current practice of examining what already is.

Journalism research

Journalism studies, as a field of research, is concerned largely with what journalism is, where it has been, and why it matters, and it tends to draw on instances of past practice to do so. Among its members are practitioners, educators, communication studies professionals, sociologists, historians, and others, who study journalism production, the artefacts created, and their reception by audiences. There is no agreed definition of journalism research, and Zelizer's (2009) five types of inquiry (sociology, history, language studies, political science and cultural analysis) sit alongside Wahl-Jorgensen and Hanitzsch's (2009) four phases of research (normative, empirical, sociological and global-comparative) and Domingo's (2008) constructivist tool kit. Meanwhile, Conboy (2013) identifies political, economic, historical, ethnographic and social science approaches to journalism research and suggests they all have validity.

There is a tendency for scholarship in the field to use analytic or critical methods to examine the attitudes of journalists, analyse journalistic products or observe what journalists do. These are all good tools for understanding what journalism is and why it is important, but they are insufficient for shaping its future. Research, according to Kopper et al. (2000), 'should not only be retrospective but should help to shape the future of journalism' (p. 511), and over the past decade several scholars have called for change in the way journalism is studied. Löffelholz (2008), for instance, argues that many of the theories common in journalism research are 'not up to the task of modelling change adequately, nor are they interested in this . . . [they] are not flexible enough to cope with the new media and communication world' (p. 24–25). Others suggest that despite the field's diversity, journalism research had become blinkered. Singer (2008) argues that there has been a narrowing of analytic and interpretative focus and that 'the underlying diversity of the intellectual tradition needs to be reclaimed' (p. 154). She suggests that new paradigms could emerge from a combination of approaches that were perhaps traditionally disparate. Writing with Quandt, she also suggests that the converged media environment 'poses a number of challenges and opportunities for journalism practitioners and scholars, who face both methodological and conceptual issues' (Quandt and Singer 2009, p. 140).

Meanwhile, Mitchelstein and Boczkowski (2009) call for theoretical renewal. They observe that the tension between tradition and change in newsrooms is also playing out in the academy as studies 'continue to apply existing lenses to look at new phenomena' (p. 575). Steensen and Ahva (2015) argue that the interdisciplinary nature of journalism research means there is a need 'to widen the scope of theoretical perspectives and approaches even further' (p. 13). And Karlsson and Strömbäck (2010) suggest 'traditional research methods are not fully applicable in a setting where the news can change continuously' (p. 15).

Amid these debates there is a view that practice itself is a valid form of knowledge production (Bacon 2006; Niblock 2007; Bacon 2011; Niblock 2012) and that journalism can be researched through practice. This view has roots in Schön's (1991) notion of reflective practice and the idea that knowledge can be produced through action. This is a relatively recent notion in journalism scholarship, and it challenges the traditional division between research and practice, where research 'denotes systematic inquiry in order to gain new knowledge, while practice is deemed to be processes employed in professional activity other than the acquisition of new knowledge' (Niblock 2012, p. 6).

This is not to say that journalism research is not evolving; it is: there are regular conferences on the future of journalism and research into journalistic practice now encompasses the use of robots, mixed reality and ambient computing. My point is that there is potential for researchers to play a greater role in driving change and exploring new possibilities rather than studying existing instances of practice. While surveys, observations and analysis of content provide insight into what journalists do and why, they do not help to develop new practice or find ways to exploit the rich, interactive and immersive experiences offered by emerging platforms.

Such a shift presents an opportunity to study technology from an enabling, proactive perspective. For journalists, this means perceiving technology as an enabler of new types of practice. This also means recognising that while technology can present new types of interactions, such as those afforded by social media, it also means journalists themselves can design interactions that not only exploit the technology but do so in a way that embodies journalistic values.

To understand journalists as enablers of technology, it is useful to study interaction design, a field that sits at the intersection of technology and people. Interaction design (IxD) seeks to create experiences that support human action. While it is concerned with the possibilities of technologies, it is also concerned with the how those possibilities fit with human behaviour and human values. As a result, it aims to create platforms, interfaces and other digital artefacts that achieve a balance between possibility and use. As a design discipline, it draws on other areas of design practice and design studies.

Design research

Design, like journalism, is both a practice and a field of study. Typically, designers address complex, ill-defined problems where there is often no clear, or single, solution and where attempts to address the problem will raise new issues. Rittel and Webber's (1973) term 'wicked problems' is often used to describe the types of issues designers tackle. The term was coined in the context of social policy, where problems can be difficult to define and are unlikely to ever be solved definitely. The term 'wicked' differentiates these types of issues from the 'tame' problems normally tackled by scientists and engineers. Design theorists such as Buchanan (1992) point out that where scientific disciplines are concerned with understanding principles, laws, rules and structures, design is universal in scope and can potentially be applied to any area of human experience. Design firms such as IDEO, for instance, use 'design thinking' to tackle complex problems in healthcare or education (Brown and Katz 2011), issues quite removed from traditional design work.

Design problems are often referred to as 'situations' or 'dilemmas' and are characterised as being 'complex enough that no correct solutions exist *a priori*' (Gaver 2012, p. 940) and as having 'too many dynamic and interconnected constraints to accurately model and control using the reductionist approach found in science and engineering' (Forlizzi et al. 2008, p. 24). Out of such complex and indeterminate subject matter, the designer seeks to invent specific and concrete proposals in the form of designs. Unlike science or engineering, design does not seek to prove or disprove a hypothesis or to produce generalised theory. Instead, it is generative: 'rather than making statements about what is, design is concerned with creating what might be' (Gaver 2012, p. 940). Design proposals represent a possibility. They are an idea for addressing an issue rather than a solution to a problem. This means design is good for things that other approaches are not.

This focus on creation is a defining aspect of design research: Jones (1992) refers to this as 'the initiation of change in manmade things' (p. 6); Bayazit (2004) describes design research as 'study, research, and investigation of the artificial made by human beings' (p. 16); and Nelson and Stolterman (2012) suggest that to create is to design, arguing that design is the first among many traditions of inquiry. Writing with Löwgren, Stolterman has also argued that the complexity of the design process and the nature of dilemmas make creativity fundamental: 'a dilemma can only be resolved by a creative leap, by transcending the limitations of the present. Since design is inevitably concerned with dilemma situations, creative thinking becomes one of the fundamental aspects of the process' (Löwgren and Stolterman 2004, p. 17).

To 'transcend the limitations of the present', designers aim to understand a given situation using qualitative methods such as interview and observation. They then draw on what they have gathered to develop design ideas through sketching and prototyping. This is followed by a process of evaluation and iteration – improving the design. This process is not about creating something universal; rather, it is about creating something unique and particular – an *ultimate particular*: 'something in the world with a specific purpose, for a specific situation, for a specific client and user, with specific functions and characteristics, and done within a limited time and with limited resources' (Stolterman 2008, p. 59). The ultimate particular carries the same dignity and importance as truth in science, but it cannot be created with a scientific approach, 'because science is a process of discerning abstractions that apply across categories or taxonomies of phenomena, while the ultimate particular is a singular and unique composition or assembly' (Nelson and Stolterman 2012, p. 31).

There is also a view in design scholarship that there is a 'designerly' way of working and interacting with situations. Cross (1982) discusses 'designerly ways of knowing' as the tacit knowledge designers bring to problem solving and the knowledge residing in designed artefacts. Stolterman too suggests that while the design literature does not provide one clear theory of design, seminal works (including Schön 1991; Cross 2001; Krippendorff 2005; Lawson 2006) 'all argue that there exists something that we can label a designerly approach, and that design is a unique human activity deserving its own intellectual treatment' (Stolterman 2008, p. 60).

Implicit here is the notion that design is different from other types of intellectual inquiry. This has meant that, at times, design has struggled to justify its practice-led approach against more rationalist methods. Cross (2001) points out that although design methods originated in science, with early scholars (Alexander 1964; Simon 1969) taking an objective and rationalist, process-focused view, this 'science of design' approach lost traction in favour of seeing design from alternative perspectives, including: as a discipline; as a form of participatory, co-operative work; and as a way of thinking. Yet the tension with science endures, stemming from whether design approaches can generate knowledge, as science does, and whether design inquiry can be considered research.

Downton (2003) notes that 'fields that employ non-quantitative modes of research have to keep re-making the case for the value of such methods in research-related contexts' (p. 71). Meanwhile, Gaver (2012) observes 'an undercurrent of questioning within the design community itself about the nature and standards of research through design' (p. 937). This uneasiness stems from concerns about a lack of clear expectations around quality and guidelines around how theory is developed. Dorst (2011) points out that there are two fundamentally different ways of looking at design: rational problem solving, which is goal-oriented; and reflective practice, a process of learning. While the rational approach is more aligned with engineering and assumes a problem can be solved, reflective practice takes its lead from Schön (1991) and his idea that knowledge can be produced through action. It follows that the outcome of that action – the artefact – contains knowledge.

Artefacts and knowledge

In practice-led research, such as design, the methods of professional practice are considered to be a form of inquiry, and the resulting artefacts are seen as an ideal or as opening a new space for research (Zimmerman et al. 2010). This does not mean that all practice is research, and scholars of practice-led research in design and in journalism agree that to be considered research, practice must contribute to knowledge and relate to the relevant theory.

In the literature on interaction design and human-computer interaction, there are several frameworks that aim to ensure that practice produces artefacts that make a contribution to knowledge. These include Research through Design (Zimmerman et al. 2007); the interaction design research triangle (Fallman 2008); concept-driven interaction design (Stolterman and Wiberg 2010); and constructive design research (Koskinen et al. 2012). Within these approaches, an artefact is produced that embodies the research undertaken and new understandings gained as a result. There is also a view that design artefacts produce intermediary forms of knowledge – knowledge that sits between theory and practice. Several forms of such knowledge have been proposed, including strong concepts (Höök and Löwgren 2012), annotated portfolios (Gaver and Bowers 2012) and bridging concepts (Dalsgaard and Dindler 2014). Such knowledge takes various forms: strong concepts are design elements; annotated portfolios are annotations of realised design examples; and bridging concepts are theoretically informed design articulations and examples.

Yet there is debate about whether artefacts themselves are sufficient to communicate what is learned through practice. Cross (1999), while noting that design knowledge exists in products, argues that to qualify as research, 'there must be reflection by the practitioner on the work, and communication of some re-usable results from that reflection' (p. 9). Similarly, Swann (2002) argues that the design process is a research process and that 'the action of designing is the same as the moment of synthesis that occurs in all forms of research, when the various parts of the data and analysis begin to make sense' (p. 55). However, he notes that this process must be made visible if it is to be recognised as research, and he makes a case for systematically documenting the design process. Gaver and Bowers (2012) argue that practice-based research might better view theory as annotation that explains designs. Solterman and Wiberg (2010) note a lack of research approaches within design that focus on theoretical advancement and are design oriented, and Fallman (2008) makes a distinction between design-oriented research (the practice of academic designers) and research-oriented design (the practice of applied researchers and designers). In his view, the result of work by this latter group is an artefact that generates general knowledge, but this is not the same as the knowledge generated by academic designers, who study designed artefacts, either in use or through bringing them into being. In this case, it is the knowledge generated through this research process that is the main contribution, and the designed artefact is a means rather than an end.

This position differs from that of Zimmerman et al. (2007), who see the creation of an artefact, designed to address a real-world issue, as a central component. In their Research through Design (RtD) approach, design is used to address wicked or complex problems, and the resulting artefact is a concrete embodiment of theory and technical opportunity. The artefact communicates design activity and facilitates knowledge transfer. Their approach draws on Nelson and Stolterman's view that design is a third research culture (distinct from science and the arts), which produces wisdom that is 'an integration of reason with observation, reflection, imagination, action, and production or making' (Nelson and Stolterman 2012, p. 18). However, like Fallman, they also differentiate research artefacts from design artefacts: research artefacts should aim to produce knowledge, so commercial implications can be de-emphasised; and research artefacts should demonstrate a significant invention. In a critique of RtD, Zimmerman and co-authors (2010) argue that knowledge implicit in an artefact hinders the development of theory and recommend a more rigorous documentation of RtD projects to facilitate the development of theory and methodology. They argue that a lack of documentation can limit the value of practice-led research contributions.

Dalsgaard and Halskov (2012) also advocate for rigorous documentation, suggesting that documenting design research acts to support reflection and provide evidence to support the insights gained as a result of the process. This is a problem in longitudinal design studies when it can be difficult to make sense of the large volumes of data that are generated. They suggest a lack of established systems or examples for documenting design research means that designers develop their own routines, but this makes it difficult to compare findings across projects. They propose a system that captures design 'events' and reflections as the process unfolds. The key point here is that the combination of process and reflection is important because as a creative practice the designers themselves play a role in the creation of the artefact and, by extension, the knowledge produced.

Designerly journalism

In journalism research the issue of knowledge production and theory development is also being debated, although discussion around practice-led approaches is less developed. Bacon has suggested that investigative and in-depth journalism meet the criteria of being 'creative and original investigation' and that the 'issue for journalism as academic research is not whether it is research, but how the nature and practice of its research is to be theorised' (Bacon 2006, p. 151).

More recently, Niblock (2012) has suggested two approaches to journalism research: theory-first and practice-first. In theory-first, the research is driven by a question that is interrogated using an appropriate methodology. Practice, in this case, is used to illustrate a point or process. In a practice-first approach, the research is driven by a problem, and practice is used to solve it. The main output is a journalistic artefact; the research is inherent within the practice; and the resulting artefact is the solution. Niblock argues that both approaches seek to advance knowledge about practice or within practice, but the benefit of a practice-first approach 'is that it permits practice from both within and without professional norms and offers a space to "test" out theoretical concepts in practice' (Niblock 2012, p. 11).

This notion of experimentation and the ability to 'imagine that-which-does-not-yet-exist' (Nelson and Stolterman 2012, p. 12) is a strength of practice-led inquiry, and one that could be better exploited to address some of the challenges facing journalism research and practice. In particular, it can go some way toward mitigating weaknesses of current methodologies, which often study what is rather than what might be. Like the wicked problems designers tackle, journalists deal with messy, unpredictable situations. Reporting or writing a news story can involve navigating a range of sources and conflicting information. On top of that, there may be ethical considerations around the impact of a story on a source, or legal challenges such as defamation. There is always a deadline, restrictions on information due to budgets, time or the willingness of sources to talk. At times there may be an editorial agenda, and there are always the demands of the medium to consider. All of these impact on a journalist's work, and they must make decisions and judgements about how best to deal with and resolve those in the interests of the reader and society more broadly. The result is a piece of journalism that accommodates these factors and is particular to the situation.

Creating these 'ultimate particulars' requires a certain amount of creativity. In design, much has been written about designerly ways of working, and the design methodologies and frameworks enable designers to accommodate the factors at play and create something new. In journalism, such frameworks for practice are less common. Instead, journalism is practiced within structures, ethics and conventions that determine things such as story formats, interactions with sources, how facts and opinions should be accommodated and whose interests should be served. These practices are so engrained that journalism is often perceived as 'overwhelmingly constrained by rules and conventions' (Fulton and McIntyre 2013, p. 18). Yet Fulton and McIntyre reveal a creative, almost designerly, approach to storytelling by practitioners: rather than constraining activity, these structures enable journalists to do their work. Journalists exercise creativity in their choice of language, style of writing, deciding who to interview and what questions to ask. The conventions and constraints of story format, ethics, news values, public interest, audience and media ownership, among others, are enabling: 'creativity is always embedded in previous works, it is always the product of a system, rather than solely attributable to an individual, and there are always structures to constrain and enable an individual in their creative process' (p. 21).

To exercise creativity, journalists make judgements. News judgement, or gut feeling, is the 'seemingly self-evident and self-explaining sense of newsworthiness' (Schultz 2007, p. 190). Newsworthiness is what determines the importance of news stories and is largely determined by news values – lists of news criteria, such as power, celebrity, magnitude or surprise. While there are several such lists (such as Galtung and Ruge 1965; Harcup and O'Neill 2001), it is also recognised that news values alone are inadequate for explaining or guiding journalistic judgment, with

O'Neill and Harcup pointing out that it is not possible to examine news values in a meaningful way 'without also paying attention to occupational routines, budgets, the market, and ideology, as well as wider global cultural, economic and political considerations' (O'Neill and Harcup 2009, p. 171). That said, judgment is a fundamental part of journalistic practice.

For Nelson and Stolterman (2012), judgement is a fundamental aspect of design and the knowledge it produces. Judgement, they argue, is at the heart of design wisdom and is 'dependent on the accumulation of the experience of consequences from choices made in complex situations' (p. 139). They distinguish between intellectual judgement (which 'may lead to an understanding of a general principle') and creative judgement (which 'leads to new concepts') and design judgement (which 'leads to a concrete particular understanding and concomitant action, within a specific contextual setting') (pp. 145–146). Journalistic judgment is like design judgement in that it is built up over time and situated in the context of the story and methods used to obtain it. Like design, journalistic methods are tools rather than strict protocols for process, and the practitioner makes judgments about how to use them in context. A designer's tools include sketching and prototyping, along with qualitative approaches such as user interviews or observations. Designers use these tools to understand the design situation and develop an idea that addresses a dilemma. There is no requirement to use specific tools; rather, the designer uses methods appropriate to the task and works within a broader iterative framework of establishing needs, designing, prototyping and evaluating. Similarly, journalists generally use qualitative tools such as interviews, observations and document analysis to gather evidence and facts on which to construct stories. Again, there are no mandated rules for using certain approaches, and the journalist chooses the best methods for the job while working within the established processes of reporting, constructing a story, editing and distribution. Like designers, journalists have creative agency, but it is often exercised within strong organisational and production constraints.

Another aspect of design practice that resonates with journalism and that is closely related to process is talk back – the idea that, during the complex process of making, the designer navigates issues and problems and these decisions have unintended consequences that impact the final outcome. In a good design process, this conversation is reflective: 'In answer to the situation's back-talk, the designer reflects-in-action on the construction of the problem, the strategies of action, or the model of the phenomena, which have been implicit in his moves' (Schön 1991, p. 79). In journalism, situation back talk is common: a complex story will seldom go smoothly, and journalists often need to navigate vested interests, secrecy, nervous sources and lies. They also negotiate the public's response, via letters to the editor, story comments, social media and complaints to regulators. As a result, the journalist might need to change the method of investigation or find a new way to tackle the story when a line of inquiry runs cold or is prevented. In such cases a journalist will reflect in action to determine the next move.

Journalism, then, is designerly. Journalists use their creativity, agency and judgement to create stories and respond to the unique characteristics of each situation. But while journalists design, journalism is not design. While it aims to reveal something new, journalism does not aim to create something new. While journalists have agency in the way they research and tell their stories, they do so within strong cultural and organisational frameworks. Also, journalistic creativity needs to be mindful of an inherent requirement to reflect reality and serve the public interest. Design, by contrast, is free to imagine possible futures, create proposals, put them out into the world and observe what happens. It is in the combination of these two practices that journalism can find space to explore and evolve.

Journalistic RtD

The NewsCube project, which is discussed in the next chapter, set out to use design methods to address a journalistic problem and generate new ideas for practice. Using Research through Design (RtD), it aimed to address the issue of journalistic hypertext and, in doing so, demonstrate how practice-led design research can lead to insights about how journalism might evolve. As mentioned earlier, RtD is a design-oriented research model that uses methods from design practice as a form of inquiry and, through the process of designing, results in the creation of an artefact that demonstrates an ideal or 'opens a new space for design' (Zimmerman et al. 2010, p. 311). Its focus on solving a real-world issue makes it logical for a discipline such as journalism that is grappling with technological disruption.

RtD has roots in 'research through art and design', described by Frayling (1993) as including work such as materials research, development work or action research. In this type of research, results and/or process are communicated separately to the designed artefact. RtD also draws on the idea that there is a designerly way of thinking and acting as distinct from scientific thinking that is good for solving wicked problems. As with Niblock's practice-as-research methodology, RtD has strong links with reflective practice. Though it is not an approach that has been applied to news design, the complex and systemic problems facing the news industry (Picard 2014), coupled with the need to innovate and invent new practice (Christensen et al. 2012), create a situation suited to design research.

In keeping with the RtD framework, the designed artefact – the NewsCube – was intended as a concrete embodiment of hypertext theory and the technical opportunity afforded by hyperlinks. The artefact aimed to communicate design activity and facilitate knowledge transfer through a transparent process of conceptualisation, designing, prototyping and evaluating. It demonstrates how a journalist-oriented researcher has deployed, documented and evaluated design techniques to extract knowledge about the future of interaction in a specific domain. Like Niblock's idea that practice can provide a space to test out theoretical concepts, the project outlined in the following chapters uses design methods to create a journalistic tool. Rather than journalism representing 'a movement towards a solution' (Niblock 2012, p. 506), it is design that provides the overarching framework and provides the new possibilities.

References

Alexander, C., 1964. *Notes on the synthesis of form*. Cambridge, MA: Harvard University Press.

Bacon, W., 2006. Journalism as research. *Australian Journalism Review*, 28 (2), 147–157.

Bacon, W., 2011. Investigative journalism in the academy-possibilities for storytelling across time and space. *Pacific Journalism Review*, 17 (1), 45.

Bayazit, N., 2004. Investigating design: A review of forty years of design research. *Design Issues*, 20 (1), 16–29.

Björgvinsson, E., 2014. Collaborative design and grassroots journalism: Public controversies and controversial publics. In: P. Ehn, E.M. Nilsson, and R. Topgaard, eds. *Making futures: Marginal notes on innovation, design, and democracy*. Cambridge, MA: MIT Press, 227–255.

Blum-Ross, A., Mills, J., Egglestone, P., and Frohlich, D., 2013. Community media and design: Insight Journalism as a method for innovation. *Journal of Media Practice*, 14 (3), 171–192.

Brown, T., 2008. Design thinking. *Harvard Business Review*, 86 (6), 84–92.

Brown, T., 2009. *Change by design: How design thinking transforms organizations and inspires innovation*. New York: Harper Collins.

Brown, T., and Katz, B., 2011. Change by design. *Journal of Product Innovation Management*, 28 (3), 381–383.

Buchanan, R., 1992. Wicked problems in design thinking. *Design Issues*, 8 (2), 5–21.

Christensen, C.M., Skok, D., and Allworth, J., 2012. Breaking news: Mastering the art of disruptive innovation in journalism. *Nieman Reports*, 66 (3), 6–20.

Conboy, M., 2013. *Journalism studies: The basics*. Oxon: Routledge.

Cross, N., 1982. Designerly ways of knowing. *Design Studies*, 3 (4), 221–227.

Cross, N., 1999. Design research: A disciplined conversation. *Design Issues*, 15 (2), 5.

Cross, N., 2001. Designerly ways of knowing: Design discipline versus design science. *Design Issues*, 17 (3), 49–55.

Dalsgaard, P., and Dindler, C., 2014. Between theory and practice: Bridging concepts in HCI research. In: M. Jones, P. Palanque, A. Schmidt, and T. Grossman, eds. *Proceedings of the SIGCHI Conference on Human Factors in Computing Systems*. New York: ACM Press, 1635–1644.

Dalsgaard, P., and Halskov, K., 2012. Reflective design documentation. In: P. Oliver and P. Wright, eds. *The designing interactive systems conference*. New York: ACM Press, 428–437.

Domingo, D., 2008. Inventing online journalism: A constructivist approach to the development of online news. In: C. Paterson and D. Domingo, eds. *Making online news*. New York: Peter Lang, 15–28.

Dorst, K., 2011. The core of 'design thinking' and its application. *Design Studies*, 32 (6), 521–532.

Downton, P., 2003. *Design research*. Melbourne: RMIT Publishing.

Fallman, D., 2008. The interaction design research triangle of design practice, design studies, and design exploration. *Design Issues*, 24 (3), 4–18.

Forlizzi, J., Zimmerman, J., and Evenson, S., 2008. Crafting a place for interaction design research in HCI. *Design Issues*, 24 (3), 19–29.

Frayling, C., 1993. Research in art and design. *Royal College of Art Research Papers*, 1 (1), 1–9.

42   Design, journalism and knowledge

Fulton, J., and McIntyre, P., 2013. Journalists on journalism: Print journalists' discussion of their creative process. *Journalism Practice*, 7 (1), 17–32.

Galtung, J., and Ruge, M.H., 1965. The structure of foreign news: The presentation of the Congo, Cuba and Cyprus crises in four Norwegian newspapers. *Journal of Peace Research*, 2 (1), 64–90.

Gaver, B., and Bowers, J., 2012. Annotated portfolios. *Interactions*, 19 (4), 40–49.

Gaver, W., 2012. What should we expect from research through design? In: J.A. Konstan, Ed H. Chi, and K. Höök, eds. *Proceedings of the SIGCHI conference on human factors in computing systems*. New York: ACM Press, 937–946.

Harcup, T., and O'Neill, D., 2001. What Is news? Galtung and Ruge revisited. *Journalism Studies*, 2 (2), 261–280.

Höök, K., and Löwgren, J., 2012. Strong concepts: Intermediate-level knowledge in interaction design research. *ACM Transactions on Computer-Human Interaction ldots*, 19 (3), 1–18.

Jones, J.C., 1992. *Design methods*. 2nd ed. New York: Van Nostrand Reinhold.

Karlsson, M., and Strömbäck, J., 2010. Freezing the flow of online news: Exploring approaches to the study of the liquidity of online news. *Journalism Studies*, 11 (1), 2–19.

Kopper, G., Kolthoff, A., and Czepek, A., 2000. Research review: Online journalism – a report on current and continuing research and major questions in the international discussion. *Journalism Studies*, 1 (3), 499–512.

Koskinen, I., Zimmerman, J., Binder, T., Redstrom, J., and Wensveen, S., 2012. *Design research through practice: from the lab, field and showroom*. San Francisco: Morgan Kaufmann.

Krippendorff, K., 2005. *The semantic turn: A new foundation for design*. Florida: CRC Press.

Lawson, B., 2006. *How designers think: The design process demystified*. Abingdon: Routledge.

Löffelholz, M., 2008. Heterogeneous – multidimensional – competing: Theoretical approaches to journalism – an overview. In: M. Löffelholz and D. Weaver, eds. *Global journalism research: theories, methods, findings, future*. Malden, MA: Wiley-Blackwell, 15–27.

Löwgren, J., 1995. Applying design methodology to software development. In: G.M. Olson and S. Schuon, eds. *Proceedings of the 1st conference on designing interactive systems: Processes, practices, methods, & techniques*. New York: ACM Press, 87–95.

Löwgren, J., and Stolterman, E., 2004. *Thoughtful interaction design: A design perspective on information technology*. Cambridge, MA: MIT Press.

Mitchelstein, E., and Boczkowski, P.J., 2009. Between tradition and change: A review of recent research on online news production. *Journalism*, 10 (5), 562–586.

Müller, R.M., and Thoring, K., 2012. Design thinking vs. lean startup: A comparison of two user-driven innovation strategies. *Leading Through Design*, 151.

Nelson, H.G., and Stolterman, E., 2012. *The design way: Intentional change in an unpredictable world.* 2nd ed. Cambridge, MA: MIT Press.

Niblock, S., 2007. From 'knowing how' to 'being able': Negotiating the meanings of reflective practice and reflexive research in journalism studies. *Journalism Practice*, 1 (1), 20–32.

Niblock, S., 2012. Envisioning journalism practice as research. *Journalism Practice*, 6 (4), 497–512.

O'Neill, D., and Harcup, T., 2009. News values and selectivity. In: K. Wahl-Jorgensen and T. Hanitzsch, eds. *The handbook of journalism studies.* New York: Routledge, 161–174.

Picard, R.G., 2014. Twilight or new dawn of journalism? Evidence from the changing news ecosystem. *Journalism Studies*, 2 (3), 273–283.

Plattner, H., Meinel, C., and Leifer, L., eds., 2015. *Design thinking research.* Cham: Springer International Publishing.

Quandt, T., and Singer, J.B., 2009. Convergence and cross-platform content production. In: K. Wahl-Jorgensen and T. Hanitzsch, eds. *The handbook of journalism studies.* New York: Routledge, 130–144.

Rittel, H.W., and Webber, M.M., 1973. Dilemmas in a general theory of planning. *Policy Sciences*, 4 (2), 155–169.

Rogers, Y., Sharp, H., and Preece, J., 2011. *Interaction design: Beyond human-computer interaction.* Hoboken, NJ: John Wiley & Sons.

Schön, D.A., 1991. *The reflective practitioner: How professionals think in action.* 2nd ed. Farnham, England: Ashgate.

Schultz, I., 2007. The Journalistic Gut Feeling: Journalistic doxa, news habitus and orthodox news values. *Journalism Practice*, 1 (2), 190–207.

Simon, H.A., 1969. *The sciences of the artificial.* Cambridge, MA: MIT Press.

Singer, J.B., 2008. Journalism research in the United States: Paradigm shift in a networked world. In: M. Löffelholz and D. Weaver, eds. *Global journalism research: Theories, methods, findings, future.* Malden, MA: Wiley-Blackwell, 145–157.

Steensen, S., and Ahva, L., 2015. Theories of journalism in a digital age: An exploration and introduction. *Digital Journalism*, 3 (1), 1–18.

Stolterman, E., 2008. The nature of design practice and implications for interaction design research. *International Journal of Design*, 2 (1), 55–65.

Stolterman, E., and Wiberg, M., 2010. Concept-driven interaction design research. *Human-Computer Interaction*, 25 (2), 95–118.

Swann, C., 2002. Action research and the practice of design. *Design Issues*, 18 (1), 49–61.

Taylor, N., Frohlich, D., Egglestone, P., Marshall, J., Rogers, J., Blum-Ross, A., Mills, J., Shorter, M., and Oliver, P., 2014. *Utilising insight journalism for community technology design*. Presented at the Proceedings of the SIGCHI Conference on Human Factors in Computing Systems, ACM Press, 2995–3004.

Wahl-Jorgensen, K., and Hanitzsch, T., 2009. Introduction: On why and how we should do journalism studies. In: K. Wahl-Jorgensen and T. Hanitzsch, eds. *The handbook of journalism studies*. New York: Routledge, 3–16.

Zelizer, B., 2009. Journalism and the academy. In: K. Wahl-Jorgensen and T. Hanitzsch, eds. *The handbook of journalism studies*. New York: Routledge, 29–41.

Zimmerman, J., Forlizzi, J., and Evenson, S., 2007. Research through design as a method for interaction design research in HCI. In: M.B. Rosson and D. Gilmore, eds. *Proceedings of SIGCHI conference on human factors in computing systems*. New York: ACM Press, 493–502.

Zimmerman, J., Stolterman, E., and Forlizzi, J., 2010. An analysis and critique of research through design: Towards a formalization of a research approach. In: O.W. Bertelsen and P. Krogh, eds. *Proceedings of the 8th ACM conference on designing interactive systems*. New York: ACM Press, 310–319.

4   NewsCube

A case of Journalism Design

Technological innovations can be confronting because they can challenge the way things are done and design artefacts, which imagine possible futures, can have a similar effect because in aiming to create something new, design artefacts aim to 'transcend' the limitations of the present. Löwgren and Stolterman (2004) point out that this is necessary because in a dilemma situation 'there is no solution hidden in the situation. Instead, a dilemma can only be resolved by a creative leap, by transcending the limitations of the present' (p. 17). Designers need to understand those limitations, but they need to show how those limitations might be overcome, challenged or disrupted. By designing an artefact, they suggest a new possibility, one that has a relationship to the current situation, but which also shows how that situation might evolve. By using the artefact and interacting with it, a person is prompted to reflect on the existing way of doing things and consider how this could change.

Design researchers use the idea of tradition and transcendence to explain this: 'we are always to some degree bound in our tradition and, at the same time, have to transcend the present in order to solve our problems' (Mogensen 1992, p. 32). In design, the process of developing, deploying and evaluating prototypes makes it possible to envisage new ways of working or thinking. These situations are not always in harmony, and tension can exist between current practice and the future practice that design artefacts make visible. One way to resolve this is to design for old skills, old values and old divisions of labour. Another is to design for the new, for what is made possible by new technologies (Ehn 1989). But there is also a space in-between. Mogensen reframes the question of what to design as *what to find out*: 'How do we on the one hand, devise qualitatively new systems, and on the other hand, ensure their usability in the given practice' (p. 32). A real strength of design, and prototyping in particular, is that the process allows you to understand how an idea can embody traditional values, processes or goals and at the same time challenge those and suggest new possibilities.

The NewsCube was an experiment in designing for transcendence. It aimed to push journalism practice in a new direction. It drew on established practices but aimed to make a creative leap in how an established technology might be used to tell stories. In doing this, it revealed the potential for physical story interactions and demonstrated how engrained attitudes to audiences and commercial concerns can hamper change. While the project borrowed the Research through Design (RtD) approach from design, the thinking that underpinned it was journalistic: I, as a former journalist, brought to the design process tacit journalistic knowledge and practices; this informed my thinking about the issue and the design and reflected a journalistic process, albeit one that did not readily map to the traditional process of reporting, story construction, editing and distribution. It is this journalistic approach to design research that makes this project distinctive and reveals how, through design, journalists might draw on their deep craft to push practice forward.

Concept to artefact

The challenge for the NewsCube project was to design a piece of technology that used hypertext in a way that allowed readers to visualise the components of a complex or long-running story and vary the perspective within them. It also aimed to design a way for journalists to more easily engage with audiences in the construction of those stories, to share control of the narrative without creating confusion. This goal called for a design that was potentially very different from the story formats commonly used in news media and so required a strong conceptual model. The conceptual model for most online news stories is a standard journalistic inverted pyramid, with hyperlinks, but simply adding links to this type of storytelling does not exploit the affordances of the underlying technology or the potential for using shape as a narrative tool.

Based on a review of the hypertext literature (Doherty 2014) and review of contemporary practice (Doherty 2013), a story cube was designed: the NewsCube. The NewsCube was essentially a virtual, three-dimensional container that could be used to aggregate, edit, create and share news content on a specific story or theme and that could be manipulated via touch gestures. The sides of the cube would provide perspectives on a story and a simple way of navigating through it. The concept aimed to exploit the familiar and tactile qualities of physical cube interfaces. It imagined a workflow in which the publisher of a news story, or a content creator, would create the cube to package a story, or collection of information, and users could contribute to and customise the cube. They could also tag or share content with the original cube such that it became an evolving, breathing story. This type of treatment would be best suited to long-running, in-depth or investigative journalism, which has multiple components and is constructed over time. The NewsCube would be a visual representation of the hyperlinks between stories. Each face of the cube could be used to cluster related content, much like a newspaper or online story package. However, these relationships would be fluid and could be changed by journalists or readers as the story evolved. Users would also be able to share cubes and link cubes together.

A key characteristic of the NewsCube idea was its ability to allow users to switch between the points of view within a narrative. Users could vary plot by categorising related content and exploring a news story from these perspectives. For example, a story about an election might be divided into categories dealing with particular policy areas, poll results or the track record of candidates. Within these categories there could be a combination of original and aggregated content from diverse sources.

While the idea of an interactive, collaborative story cube is unique in journalism, a cube itself is by no means an original invention. Any set of children's building blocks would be deficient without this common geometric shape, and the Rubik's Cube was a hugely successful toy. But the simplicity of the form masks features that make the cube a fascinating and particularly interactive shape, and cubes have been used in interactive media. Research projects include Display Blocks (Pla and Maes 2012), pCubee (Stavness et al. 2010), Navigational Blocks (Camarata et al. 2002), The Cubic Mouse (Fröhlich and Plate 2000), ToolStone (Rekimoto and Sciammarella 2000), and mediaBlocks (Ullmer and Ishii 1999). These projects deal with physical cubes, or rectangular blocks in some cases, and explore the shape as a way to navigate, transport or input data to a computer. While these projects do not address shape as a narrative device, they provide some insight into the affordances of cubes and suggest that beyond their simple geometry, cubes have qualities of playfulness, perspective, familiarity, extensibility and ease of manipulation – all qualities that could be exploited for telling news stories with greater interactivity.

With a conceptual model in mind, I began designing the News-Cube. I have written about this process previously (see Doherty 2015, 2017), so here I will describe briefly the design process and some of the key design artefacts and how they embodied journalistic practice, before discussing how the NewsCube led to the concept of Journalism Design.

The design process

The process of interaction design typically begins with contextual research, where the dilemma and problem space are investigated. This often involves a combination of desk research and user studies. Interview and observation are common techniques, and researchers aim to develop an understanding of the potential users of a design and the context in which the artefact will be deployed. The next phase is designing. Here, techniques such as sketching, wireframing and prototyping are used to bring concepts to a form that can elicit feedback. All of these outputs are design artefacts. Of these artefacts, prototypes are the most valuable for research. Prototypes embody the knowledge and understanding the designer gains as a result of the process of bringing them into existence. Evaluation follows, and normally prototypes are given to potential users who provide feedback that can be used to improve the design.

While I have described these phases in sequence, it should be noted that design, like any creative process, rarely follows a linear path, and certainly within this broader cycle the process can track backward, jump forward or involve several smaller design cycles. Figure 4.1 shows the design process used in the NewsCube project. It involved the phases common in interaction design and used a range of qualitative and practice-based methods, including interviews, observation, sketching and prototyping.

I carried out the contextual research and initial design work on my own but worked with developers to create the initial prototype and later beta version. Both iterations were evaluated with the help of ten research participants, who used the tool and were interviewed about their experience. The participants, eight in the first round and two later, were all employed in journalism or the digital publishing industry. They are identified here via pseudonyms: Charlie and Shannon were interaction designers at a national broadcaster, and they worked in separate units in different cities; Tyler, Val and James worked in a range of roles at a publishing start-up; Dale was a communication consultant and former newspaper editor; Alex was the digital editor at a metropolitan daily newspaper; Riley was a freelance journalist and communications consultant; and Max and Drew were the managing editor and production manager of the digital news division of a national broadcaster. I have called the developers Sam and Chris.

Through their comments, the participants reveal things not only about the NewsCube but also about themselves and the context in

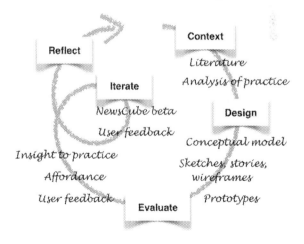

Figure 4.1 The design process used to create the NewsCube.

Source: author.

which they work. This is one of the strengths of design: that through artefacts, or prototypes, researchers can probe situations to learn more about the people and technologies involved. This knowledge is used to develop ideas about how to redesign the artefact to better suit the situation or to design new artefacts to prompt change in the situation. In this way, design artefacts can help reveal how current practices might evolve. Lim and co-authors have discussed design artefacts, and prototypes in particular, as 'design-thinking enablers' and as 'tools for traversing a design space' (Lim et al. 2008, p. 2), and that was certainly the case in the creation of the NewsCube.

Throughout the process of designing and prototyping, several design artefacts were created, including sketches, wireframes and stories. These played an important role in communicating ideas, passing on knowledge, and facilitating thinking. For instance, sketches created on a whiteboard during a scoping meeting with Sam and Chris were crucial to working through and understanding the lifecycle of a NewsCube: how it was created, filled, organised and shared. While some of these issues had been addressed in a briefing document, talking about them, describing the process and sketching the interaction between users, content and interface raised new issues, such as who owned a NewsCube and who controlled it. In a traditional news paradigm, these are not generally topics of concern: publishers and broadcasters own stories and control them. But in a digital ecosystem it is not so clear cut, and a series of quick disposable drawings helped work through issues such as who owned the cube, how to deal with more than six categories (reflecting the sides of the cube), and who has control of a public cube. In addressing the issue of ownership, for instance, I began with tradition and explained how a news organisation would moderate comments on a story it published, mindful of legal and ethical constraints. I then considered the technological possibility: that readers could be involved in story construction and could change the narrative. This led to the assumption that the NewsCube would need a similar process and that the creator of a cube would become its owner and have additional control.

This understanding in turn informed the design of wireframes, which gave structure and function to the initial conceptual model. The process of making wireframes – skeletal drawings of the NewsCube iPad prototype – revealed issues of visualisation and navigation. For instance, the simplicity of the cubic shape obscures a complex network of links and annotations on the inside of the cube; how, given limited screen size, could this be explained to readers? While this problem was not solved definitively, it illustrates the challenge of striking a balance between what is envisaged in a design and what can be achieved within the bounds of budget, skill, time and technical possibility. Together, these design artefacts led to the development of a prototype: a concrete manifestation of the design concept.

Prototypes

There were three key versions of the NewsCube prototype: a low-fidelity prototype; a digital, iPad prototype; and a Web-based beta version. These prototypes represented iterations of the design: conceptual model; research prototype; and translation. Of these, the second was the most important in terms of understanding how journalistic practice might change.

The design work underpinning the NewsCube began with a pair of balsa wood cubes (figure 4.2) onto which were glued paper images on the theme of coal seam gas. One cube displayed images

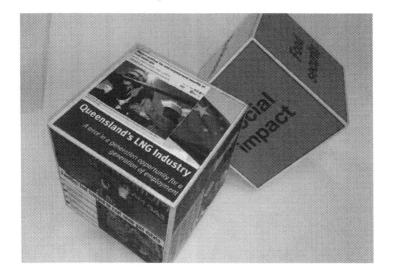

Figure 4.2 Balsa wood cubes which captured the NewsCube conceptual model.
Source: author.

and text from news sites, reports, and social media, among other sources. The second showed possible categories, or ways of labelling the cube faces. These cubes were used in the scoping meeting, mentioned above, to communicate the design concept. They would be considered low-fidelity prototypes: they were cheap and fast to construct; focused on the look and feel of the interface; contained no functionality; and were constructed to communicate and inform, rather than form the basis for developing code (Rudd et al. 1996). This meant they were effective for communicating the idea that a news story would be displayed on six surfaces and that content could be grouped thematically on each side as well as via links between sides. The prototypes essentially captured the design's conceptual model and illustrated how data would be represented. In this sense, they were the 'right fidelity for their purpose' (Buxton 2007, p. 295). From a journalistic perspective, they clearly reflected established ways of organising content, both online and in print. But they provided a high-level concept of how that established practice might be adapted to a new format.

The digital iPad prototype (figure 4.3) progressed this idea and showed how a virtual cube might work in practice. A large

Figure 4.3 The iPad prototype could be manipulated via touch.

Source: author.

cube dominated the design, and users could create a NewsCube, manipulate it with their fingers, add and annotate content, and create relationships between individual items via links. Although not fully implemented, the prototype suggested the ability for collaboration. A public/private button enabled users to make their News-Cubes visible to other participants, and inactive buttons on the content creation pane suggested the ability to incorporate social media. This mixed fidelity model (McCurdy et al. 2006) meant that users could experience a substantial depth of functionality for the core tasks (creating hypertexts) and a rich experience interacting with the cube interface. The prototype was less highly developed in its breadth of functionality, such as the inactive social media and sharing functionality, and in its level of visual refinement – the NewsCube was black and white and did not have any graphical design.

This prototype was the point at which the design process intersected with the journalistic process in a concrete way – i.e. the NewsCube was used to tell a story. During development of this prototype, a complementary journalistic process was underway to generate content. The NewsCube was conceived to package long-running or complex journalism topics. So began a process of reporting and aggregating content for three NewsCubes on the issues of soil security, new anti-association laws and technology news. Adding content to the prototype revealed a fresh insight into the potential of the NewsCube: that it could be used as a reporting tool as well as a storytelling tool, and that a NewsCube would evolve over time. This was a new insight that came as a result of doing, and reflecting on, journalism. While the idea of a journalist sharing a cube with users was part of the initial concept, the idea that the cube could evolve with the journalist's own reporting process was new.

The third iteration was the Web-based beta (figure 4.4). This version was created thanks to an Australian industry grant: the NewsCube won an inaugural Walkley Grant for Innovation in Journalism. One of the requirements of the grant was to create a responsive Web-based version of the tool, the logic being that this would make it easier for the platform to scale to a broader user base than would be possible if it was only accessible to users of Apple's iOS platform. This meant diverging from the tactility of the tablet-based prototype, and it also meant that the redesign was

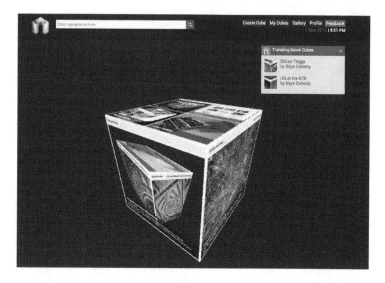

Figure 4.4 Screenshot from the NewsCube beta website at http://newscube.io.
Source: author.

constrained in its ability to explore alternatives to the cube concept. However, this version did offer the opportunity to refine parts
of the prototype (sharing and collaboration were implemented)
and evaluate it further. This phase of the project goes some way
toward illustrating the tension between design as exploration and
design as product development. I will return to this point in the
next chapter.

The creation of these prototypes illustrate an important point
about design and help build the case for Journalism Design: the
design process was not only underpinned by journalistic thinking;
it also enabled journalistic thinking in a new context – that is, in
the design of technology. Through conceptualising and designing
the NewsCube I, the journalist was forced to apply journalistic
practice in a novel situation and consider the consequences of that
new practice. For instance, the process of creating story cubes
for the iPad prototype raised issues of control and workflow. The
developers needed to understand how the editing process would

be controlled in a collaborative cube and when an annotation would be added. I sought to resolve these issues by drawing on tradition, by returning to formats, conventions and constraints of journalism practice – for example, the relationship between two pieces of information might not be immediately obvious and could emerge through the process or reporting, so it would be important to be able to create links or add annotations at any time. Because the NewsCube could capture this journalistic process, it could function as a tool both for facilitating journalistic thinking and for revealing that thinking to a reader. Yet it was also an application for story consumption and collaboration, and that meant there would need to be a point at which the journalist relinquished control. This combination of production and consumption would enable the story to be taken further by the readers and in this way asks them to think 'journalistically'.

In this way the process of designing revealed an underlying reflection-in-action (Schön 1991). The knowledge produced as a result was fed back into the design process and embodied in the artefacts. The approach taken here resembles Niblock's practice-first approach, in that the research was driven by a problem, in this case how to better exploit hypertext. But instead of journalism representing 'a movement towards a solution' (Niblock 2012, p. 506), it was design that provided the overarching framework for practice and that provided new possibilities for journalism. It was a design process that led to the idea of a virtual storytelling cube and was a design process that enabled that idea to develop into a prototype.

Beyond capturing design research, prototypes are artefacts for use, and it is though use that the social value of a design becomes evident. Prototypes are a way to probe a situation and examine practice. Wensveen and Matthews (2015) suggest that 'anything that treats design as an intervention in the world and studies its consequences, or work that deploys prototypes in the field and analyses their use' (p. 268), works in this way. This type of information is valuable in design because it provides insight into the context of use. In the case of the NewsCube, it was through using and reflecting on the designed prototype that journalists and news designers were able to perceive new possibilities for storytelling and interaction as well as barriers.

User feedback

The cube is a tricky shape to work with in a journalistic context. Ostensibly its qualities do not meet an obvious need. Its playfulness, perspective, familiarity, extensibility and ease of manipulation that characterise it as a cube are great for interactivity, but, as the journalism ethnographers tell us, this is an industry grappling with the technical and cultural challenges brought about by digital technologies. The most pressing needs are retaining audiences and revenues, and an interactive cube is an unlikely panacea.

Feedback on the NewsCube prototype covered a range of topics, among them the playfulness and interactivity of the interface, its fidelity, potential for storytelling and difficulty of use. But the most dominant themes centred on shape and issues of ownership. These are closely related: the shape of the prototype gave the users a feeling of control over it. It was like a building block that could be manipulated; it was tactile and responsive. But it also made demands on users that they did not anticipate: there were only six sides, but they set up an expectation that the cube needed to be filled. At the same time, the influence of commercial considerations and views of the audience emerged as barriers to transcending traditional practice.

Intention, perception, shape

The NewsCube is a cube because it was designed to bound hyperspace, to make it navigable and to facilitate storytelling from multiple perspectives. It also aimed to design a way for journalists to more easily engage with audiences in the construction of those stories, to share control of the narrative without creating confusion. These were its intentions and formed the core of the conceptual model on which the design was developed. However, the shape proved to be simultaneously the NewsCube's strongest feature and biggest challenge. On the one hand, it was familiar and interactive; on the other, it made demands that other story formats did not.

To some extent, feedback on the iPad prototype validated the conceptual model. Most of the participants understood that they could use the NewsCube to create hyperlinked stories that were organised around different perspectives. Using the balsa wood prototype to explain the concept before deploying the digital prototype helped in this regard. For Dale the shape mapped easily to journalistic ways of organising information, and for Riley it allowed her to take a reader through a chain of reasoning. And although Tyler found it difficult to think about topics from six perspectives, he grasped the concept. But the idea did not resonate with all. For instance, Shannon's mental model of how to organise and synthesise content did not map well to a cube, and she did not see value in the interface. Although the cube afforded six points of view, with the intention of providing a big picture view of a story, she could see only one face at a time and so did not perceive that affordance.

This was not the only time when the perceptions of users did not match the intention of the designer. The ability to add up to nine items to each side was intended to allow scope for exploration, but users instead perceived a task that had to be completed. Similarly, the idea of collaboration intended a NewsCube to become an evolving, constructive hypertext. While users saw potential in collaboration, they also perceived the shape to be ideal for storage and archiving – for stasis, not evolution – and not intended.

This disconnect might be explained in part by the fidelity of the prototype. As mentioned earlier, the NewsCube was a mixed-fidelity prototype, and collaboration was one function that was rendered in low-fidelity: the possibility was suggested but not implemented. So, while users had a rich experience interacting with the interface, which was reflected in the comments and insights about the shape and its tactility, feedback on its collaborative intention was speculative and, in some cases, based on previous experience rather than use of the prototype. Another intention of the shape was to bound the space in which a hyperlinked story could exist and so help structure information and aid comprehension. While users did perceive affordances such as perspective, context, synthesis and comprehension, which reflected those intentions, they did not see them all as positive. Rather than provide navigation, the shape was perceived as restricting the ability to explore. Similarly, although the NewsCube could accommodate more content than any of the users added to it, there was a perception that the shape limited the scope of a story.

Yet throughout the project, the conceptual model remained consistent: a virtual, three-dimensional cube. As the NewsCube evolved from rudimentary prototype to functioning, responsive website, grappling with the demands of the shape were constant. In the balsa wood prototypes, the physicality of the cube was the key feature. This translated fairly well to an iPad prototype because it was a defined size and people still used their hands to manipulate it. But on the Web, tactility is mediated by a mouse or trackpad, and the size changes depending on the size of the user's screen. So, while a Web version meant the design was more usable in terms of creating content, the tactile qualities were lost.

Insight to practice

As a probe into practice, the NewsCube revealed aspects of culture and practice that could restrict the ability of journalists to exploit the affordances they identified. Among the challenges were the need for narrative control, the influence of commercial objectives, and views on the role of the audience. On the other hand, the NewsCube prompted ideas around distributed control, physical interactions and emotional engagement with stories through their design, as opposed to content.

Whether they were concerned about narratives, audiences, or journalism more generally, all the participants discussed how the NewsCube challenged control in some way. There were concerns about how the ability for collaboration would impact editorial integrity and comprehension, with Riley pointing out the challenge of controlling narrative: 'you want your reader to have a certain amount of freedom but on the other hand you want to guide them through.' There was also reluctance to linking to diverse sources, which may be external to the publisher, underscoring a tendency within journalism to view hypertext as a way to retain readers rather than a tool for narrative construction.

Some did not see strategic benefits in using hyperlinks because of the way news organisation counted them. These types of comments illustrate the influence of commercial objectives in decisions about storytelling and engagement. For instance, two participants, Dale and Alex, worked at different times at the same news commercial organisation and had different performance indicators: traffic and time. This meant their use of hyperlinks had little to do with the narrative or interactive affordances and more about meeting targets. For Drew and Max at the national broadcaster, however, diversity was valued, and they were seeking to add interactivity and atmosphere to stories. For them the ability for exploration was valuable. This suggests that any new idea for storytelling and audience engagement will need to fit with an organisation's strategic goals.

There were mixed views about the role of readers. Some saw them as passive; others welcomed the idea of collaborative story making. Certainly the participants did acknowledge that the relationship between journalists and audiences had changed and that there was a need for greater engagement. This was particularly strong at the national broadcaster where the desire to address different user behaviours on various platforms was becoming unsustainable: 'you've got all these on and off platforms, if you like, experiences that each have different user behaviours and different market segments and you know the ideal scenario is that you are taking one story and tailoring it for each of those. And that becomes very labour intensive very quickly.'

However, understanding news audiences was a challenge in itself. Dale pointed out that traditional practice did not provide journalists the opportunity to understand their audiences or communities. In his view, this meant there was a disconnect between products and readers: 'I think one of the big problems that journalists have is actually working out how the real world lives. [. . .] I think it is a real challenge for journalists to actually see their audience and understand the audience. I don't know how many journalists want to do that.'

New possibilities

Despite cultural challenges, the NewsCube revealed new possibilities for the distributed control of stories. The participants all liked the physical control they had over a cube, and this reinforced their sense of ownership over a story; however, there was an awareness that the NewsCube would be more effective if others were involved. Tyler, for instance, tried to use the NewsCube to tell a story about an elaborate hacking in Japan that sent police on a wild chase, arresting innocent people. He had been following the story for some time and had collected all the information about it that he could find. He had hoped that creating a NewsCube would reveal new connection between the facts, but it did not: 'I didn't ever feel I'd gained a new understanding, but maybe that's because I'd been following it so intensely that I already had a good understanding.' What he needed was collaboration: 'I could have put that out there and said "hey I'm really interested in info on this can anyone who reads Japanese share some translated articles on the cube, or something."'

Similarly, Riley thought that relinquishing some level of narrative control could allow for greater interaction, and she imagined she could invite readers to join her in analysis of complex policy areas. She was prepared to relinquish some narrative control in return for a better outcome. Certainly, collaboration raises new challenges for journalism, particularly around the idea of exclusivity and the notion of a 'scoop'.

News experiences that involve physical interaction were another idea provoked by the prototype. Nearly all the participants liked the physical qualities of the NewsCube. They liked the way they could manipulate it, and Dale made the point that the tactility was reminiscent of a newspaper, suggesting the potential for new designs that exploit some of the qualities of traditional media – rather than adapting third-party platforms to journalistic purposes, there could be value in embracing some of those traditions and designing new interactions for them.

Playfulness emerged as another driver of new news experiences. The fun, familiar characteristics of the NewsCube are qualities that are not readily associated with hard news or current affairs, but many of the participants noted how they enjoyed the experience. These qualities were driven by the cube shape and the tactility of the interface. It is worth noting that playfulness was not something that was intended in the design, but it is certainly something that could be consciously designed for. Charlie pointed out the strong psychological effect of playfulness and suggested it was a quality that might be attractive to younger audiences. This type of insight suggests there is potential for thinking about stories as experiences.

Exploration and the ability to discover new things was another quality that emerged as valuable. After using the Web version, Drew pointed out that 'finding out about stuff at your own pace' was an attraction of digital platforms. He pointed out that immersion, playfulness and atmosphere were qualities he was trying to instil in stories as a way of counterbalancing the 'seriousness' of news. It is interesting to note the idea of emotion that emerges from the NewsCube as a design prototype is quite different from traditional notions of surprise, conflict or bad news that govern the prominence of news stories. Where traditionally journalists have used the telling of human suffering or pleasure to engage readers emotionally with stories, it was the NewsCube's interface that drove an affective response from the participants – they enjoyed the experience; playing with the cube was pleasurable.

While Max and Drew were focused on the user experience and recognised that news organisations needed to respond to user behaviour, there appeared to be an emphasis on adapting news delivery to the requirements of various social and mobile platforms. This was challenging and something the newsroom was struggling with. It is possible that this struggle was driven in part by strong links to traditional practice, in particular a reliance on news articles as the key delivery mechanism: each platform required a different style of article, and these required intensive labour to create. So while there appeared to be an experimental attitude, this was centred on adapting existing outputs to evolving technology. A proactive approach might be more effective. This might involve designing new outputs for evolving technologies or designing new technology and new outputs.

Designing for transcendence

As discussed earlier, Rogers (2006) advocates for a shift away from proactive technologies that drive human action to a focus on proactive people and creating user experiences that 'extend what people currently do' (p. 406). Ubiquitous computing technologies, she argues, should be developed for particular domains rather than generic users. It is here that deep domain knowledge – Arthur's deep craft (Arthur 2011) – combined with technical understanding can enable journalists to design innovative news experiences that embody their core tenets of practice. It is this junction that underpins the notion of Journalism Design. It is an approach that draws on both journalism and interaction design and aims to push those practices in unfamiliar directions, thereby revealing how to transcend established practices.

The NewsCube took the journalistic reporting process and conventions for telling stories, combined them with theories of hypertext, and proposed a three-dimensional, interactive and collaborative interface. The result was a design that was related to the current situation yet challenged some established practices and opened the possibility for tangible, playful interactions that gave readers some control over a story. While the feedback revealed a willingness on the part of journalists to relinquish some level of editorial control in return for greater audience engagement, strong commercial demands emerged as an impediment to change within news organisations. Comments from Dale and Alex, in particular, reveal the impact of a business's internal measures of success on the extent to which editorial staff might experiment with new formats: Dale was motivated to engage with niche audiences, while Alex chased 'junk traffic'. So while individual journalists might be willing to involve readers in collaborative storytelling or experiment with greater tactility, such activities may not result in measures that meet business goals. This raises a new issue: how to reimagine editorial control given the new media ecosystem.

In the context of a challenging business environment, there is a need to experiment with new ideas even if they do not produce a return. This is the 'innovators dilemma' that Christensen and co-authors (2012) say mires news companies: new entrants are stealing audiences and revenues from legacy organisations, which are reluctant to take a chance on change. Design can help mitigate some of this risk. As has been shown here, the process of designing something, deploying it into the world and evaluating it reveals new possibilities and how current practice might hamper those possibilities.

As a design probe, the NewsCube reveals that designs that reduce a journalist's control over the storytelling process can be confronting. However, it also tells us that there is new value to be found in designing stories for physical, affective interaction and for greater collaboration. Journalists have considered these things before: games, for instance, have long been part of the newspaper experience (Bogost et al. 2010), and social networks (Hille and Bakker 2013) have been used to collaborate with audiences and distribute reporting work. But through design, we can understand the implications of a new idea or a new technology on the people involved.

In this way, the designed artefact played an important role in revealing to the participants aspects of their own practice that would need to change to fully exploit three-dimensional, cubic storytelling. The artefact probed their practice, and, through interacting with it, and reflecting on it, the participants perceived possibilities for transcending their traditions. The ideas of distributed control, physicality and emotion emerged as paths for moving beyond the limits of established practice and creating new ways of working. In this way Journalism Design draws on the reflective, iterative and problem-solving qualities of design research to probe situations and reveal new ways of thinking about and changing them. It suggests a way for research to 'permit practice from both within and without professional norms' and to offer 'a space to "test" out theoretical concepts in practice' (Niblock 2012, p. 11). It shows the benefits of practice-led inquiry to imagine things that do not yet exist (Nelson and Stolterman 2012), and it enables journalism research to 'help shape the future of journalism' (Kopper et al. 2000, p. 511).

Yet the work here is to some extent constrained by its relationship to traditional journalism: the NewsCube was tied to established ideas of story construction and dissemination, and the insights gained were constrained by the experiences and organisational drivers of those involved. The logical next step is to remove those constraints and design not for journalistic processes but for core principles and values.

References

Arthur, W.B., 2011. *The nature of technology: What it is and how it evolves.* New York: Free Press.

Bogost, I., Ferrari, S., and Schweizer, B., 2010. *Newsgames: Journalism at play.* MIT Press.

Buxton, B., 2007. *Sketching user experiences: Getting the design right and the right design.* San Francisco: Morgan Kaufmann.

Camarata, K., Do, E.Y-L., Johnson, B.R., and Gross, M.D., 2002. Navigational blocks: navigating information space with tangible media. In: K. Hammond, Y. Gil, and D. Leake, eds. *Proceedings of the 7th international conference on intelligent user interfaces.* New York: ACM Press, 31–38.

Christensen, C.M., Skok, D., and Allworth, J., 2012. Breaking news: Mastering the art of disruptive innovation in journalism. *Nieman Reports*, 66 (3), 6–20.

Doherty, S., 2013. Hypertext and news stories, *ITEE Technical Report No. 2013-03*. Brisbane, Australia: School of Information Technology and Electrical Engineering, The University of Queensland. 1–10.

Doherty, S., 2014. Hypertext and journalism: Paths for future research. *Digital Journalism*, 2 (2), 124–139.

Doherty, S., 2015. NewsCubed: Journalism through design. *Journalism Practice*, 1–20.

Doherty, S., 2017. *Journalism design: The NewsCube, interactive technologies and practice*. PhD Thesis. University of Queensland, Brisbane.

Ehn, P., 1989. *Work-oriented design of computer artifacts*. Stockholm: Arbetslivscentrum.

Fröhlich, B., and Plate, J., 2000. The cubic mouse: A new device for three-dimensional input. In: T. Turner and G. Szwillus, eds. *Proceedings of the SIGCHI conference on human factors in computing systems*. New York: ACM Press, 526–531.

Hille, S., and Bakker, P., 2013. I like news: searching for the 'Holy Grail' of social media. *European Journal of Communication*, 28 (6), 663–680.

Kopper, G., Kolthoff, A., and Czepek, A., 2000. Research review: Online journalism – a report on current and continuing research and major questions in the international discussion. *Journalism Studies*, 1 (3), 499–512.

Lim, Y-K., Stolterman, E., and Tenenberg, J., 2008. The anatomy of prototypes: Prototypes as filters, prototypes as manifestations of design ideas. *ACM Transactions on Computer-Human Interaction*, 15 (2), 1–27.

Löwgren, J., and Stolterman, E., 2004. *Thoughtful interaction design: A design perspective on information technology*. Cambridge, MA: MIT Press.

McCurdy, M., Connors, C., Pyrzak, G., Kanefsky, B., and Vera, A., 2006. Breaking the fidelity barrier: An examination of our current characterization of prototypes and an example of a mixed-fidelity success. In: R. Grinter, T. Rodden, P. Aoki, Ed Cuttrell, R. Jefferies and G. Olson, eds. *Proceedings of the SIGCHI conference on human factors in computing systems*. New York: ACM Press, 1233–1242.

Mogensen, P.H., 1992. Towards a provotyping approach in systems development. *Scandinavian Journal of Information Systems*, 4, 31–53.

Nelson, H.G., and Stolterman, E., 2012. *The design way: intentional change in an unpredictable world*. 2nd ed. Cambridge, MA: MIT Press.

Niblock, S., 2012. Envisioning journalism practice as research. *Journalism Practice*, 6 (4), 497–512.

Pla, P., and Maes, P., 2012. Display blocks: Cubic displays for multi-perspective visualization. In: J.A. Konstan, Ed H Chi and K. Höök, eds.

CHI'12 Extended abstracts on human factors in computing systems. New York: ACM Press, 2015–2020.

Rekimoto, J., and Sciammarella, E., 2000. Toolstone: effective use of the physical manipulation vocabularies of input devices. In: M. Ackerman and K. Edwards, eds. *Proceedings of the 13th annual ACM symposium on user interface software and technology*. New York: ACM Press, 109–117.

Rogers, Y., 2006. Moving on from Weiser's vision of calm computing: Engaging ubicomp experiences. In: *International conference on ubiquitous computing*. New York: Springer, 404–421.

Rudd, J., Stern, K., and Isensee, S., 1996. Low vs. high-fidelity prototyping debate. *Interactions*, 3 (1), 76–85.

Schön, D.A., 1991. *The reflective practitioner: How professionals think in action*. 2nd ed. Farnham, England: Ashgate.

Stavness, I., Lam, B., and Fels, S., 2010. pCubee: A perspective-corrected handheld cubic display. In: E. Mynatt, G. Fitzpatrick, S. Hudson, K. Edwards, and T. Rodden, eds. *Proceedings of the SIGCHI conference on human factors in computing systems*. New York: ACM Press, 1381–1390.

Ullmer, B., and Ishii, H., 1999. MediaBlocks: tangible interfaces for online media. In: M.E. Atwood, ed. *CHI '99 Extended abstracts on human factors in computing systems*. New York: ACM Press, 31–32.

Wensveen, S., and Matthews, B., 2015. Prototypes and prototyping in design research. In: P.A. Rodgers and J. Yee, eds. *Routledge companion to design research*. London: Routledge, 262–262.

5   Reimagining journalism

Since completing the NewsCube project, I have begun to think that to imagine the future of journalism, it could be useful to imagine it without the trappings of journalism – that is, journalism removed from its established processes, organisational structures and embedded formats; journalism separate from deadlines, newsrooms and maybe even news. Perhaps this is a radical idea: what is journalism without news? But perhaps news is not the only product the practice of journalism can produce.

Projects such as Bespoke (Blum-Ross et al. 2013; Taylor et al. 2014) and grassroots media initiatives in Sweden (Björgvinsson 2014) tell us how journalism might be applied in different domains and how journalism might work as part of community-focused design projects. From a business perspective, Anand (2016) makes the point that connections with people are more important than content and that efforts to preserve content can mean other opportunities are lost. Yet discovering those opportunities can be a challenge and, once discovered, a new opportunity can be disruptive. The key lesson from the NewsCube project was that in proposing a new idea we can perceive new possibilities, and while those possibilities can encompass aspects of established practice, they will also reveal new opportunities. The question then is which traditions are important, and necessary, to transcendence. My answer is core values. If we take journalism's deep craft – social responsibility, the public interest – and combine it with emerging technologies, what might emerge? This is not about adapting technology to existing practice, or vice versa; it is about the synergy between the two and about proactive practice.

In my classroom over the past five years, I have encouraged students to design for transcendence. I have suggested that just because journalism has become operationalised in a newsroom and creates outputs called news stories, it does not mean this is the only way to commit acts of journalism. I ask them to think about technologies, think about what is important about journalism, and to design interactions that achieve those goals. They use a design process and reflect on what they have learned. What is emerging is a sense of optimism and excitement and, through design concepts and reflections, an agenda for Journalism Design is emerging.

Journalism + interaction design

The Journalism Design course (JxD) introduces interaction design to final-year journalism students. The course began as a cross-faculty collaboration: students studying journalism in the humanities and social sciences faculty teamed up with students studying interaction design from the engineering and information technology faculty. Together they researched, designed and prototyped a new idea for journalism (Angus and Doherty 2015). Projects explored how virtual reality, augmented reality, gaming and physical computing, among others, might be used in a journalistic context. Journalism students tended to provide domain and fieldwork expertise, while the design students contributed methodological and technical skills. Between them, the teams created functioning digital prototypes of their ideas.

In the best teams, the students' skills sets were complementary, and they learned from each other, conceiving ideas that were a marriage of journalistic practices and technical possibility. But this was not always the case, and there was a tendency for the journalism students to perceive innovation as dependent upon those with technical abilities, to see journalism as providing content for new interactive platforms, rather than the other way round: that technology could be a driver of new journalistic experiences. So I redesigned the course.

The new iteration focuses on the junction of journalistic values, technical possibility and the context of use. The collaboration was unwound and the journalism students no longer collaborate with IT students. The course now has a stronger emphasis on design methods to generate and communicate ideas. Sketching is used to explore possibilities and inform a design concept, which is proto-typed using low-fidelity methods such as storyboards, interactive wireframes or cardboard. This means the focus is on the idea and how it embodies or challenges core journalistic values rather than on functionality or technical implementation. Design research is required throughout the project and students are encouraged to understand users and give their prototype to these people and seek feedback. At the end of the process they reflect on their arte-fact and consider what they have learned about journalism. This approach sees journalistic values as a way of encouraging ideas that are particular to journalism practice rather than concepts that could simply be applied to journalistic practice.

Dozens of projects have emerged. Students have explored the possibilities for wearable journalism, technologies that could make conflict reporting safer, ways to engage young people in political news and platforms for collaboration between citizen and professional journalists. Sometimes the projects start with a tech-nology – virtual reality, drones, robots, sensors, for example. In these types of projects, the focus is on how journalism might be designed for these technologies and how the technologies change journalism. In other projects, the emphasis is on a journalistic or social goal, and technology is used to help imagine an improved situation. Such projects exist in a hybrid, or shared, space between journalism, social design and public communication.

In the FashTrack project, for example, the students wanted to investigate the junction of mobile quick response codes (QR codes) and fashion journalism. They conceived an application that allowed users to scan clothing labels and access a database of the ethical credentials of various fashion brands. Their aim was to deliver the story behind the clothing and enable consumers to make informed choices at the point of sale. Their design concept included stories and visualisations to communicate ethical fashion issues, which differentiated it from ethical shopping apps. Their prototype was created using freely available software for interac-tive wireframes. Johnston (2016) has noted the potential for public relations to enable society to make informed choices, and this pro-ject, though positioned in journalism practice, would not be out of place in some areas of public relations.

The Mobile Media project could easily fall under a social design umbrella. The project aimed to deliver news and information to homeless people. Recognising that those who struggle to find somewhere to live often do not have easy access to the internet or mobile communications, the team devised a concept for a physical computer hub that would travel alongside an established mobile laundry service that serviced the city's homeless population. They envisaged a simplified computer interface that provided links to government services and support services as well as an individual account that allowed users to download and store files that they could access the next time they used the mobile computer service. The idea, communicated via a cardboard model and wireframes of the interface, was to address the practical, everyday information needs of those disconnected from regular flows of mass and social media. This emphasis on news and information positions the project as journalistic; however, a focus on the needs of a particular 'public' with a view to helping create a different future for that public resonates with work in social design (Le Dantec 2016).

Another project, Civical, imagined journalism embedded in the built environment as a way to combat news bias and algorithmic tailoring. The team behind this project was concerned about political apathy among young adults and sought a way to make visible the relationships between public policy and the city's young inhabitants. They designed a Pokémon Go-style application in which users learned about policy decisions, public spending and political support behind the construction of public buildings, bridges, roads and the like. To evaluate the idea, they designed a prototype focused on the university and the promises made by candidates about student services in an upcoming student election. Information was mapped to buildings and services on campus, and each user's story built up as they discovered more. Sketches and interactive wireframes were used to develop and evaluate the idea.

Although quite disparate, these projects demonstrate how journalism might evolve if it is decoupled from some of its organisational and structural constraints. Indeed, few of the ideas involved a newsroom in any way. Instead, they relied on journalistic principles and values and applied them in new contexts that were sometimes shared by other practices. A common thread here was the notion of a public or community that was being served or whose issues were being addressed. What was distinctive in these projects was the focus on technology and how technologies enable journalism. Through the design process, the students found a way to imagine new possibilities and to give substance to those ideas via prototypes. As I discussed earlier, it is the process of creating and reflecting that enables design practice to lead to new insights and knowledge. To this end the students were encouraged to extract meaning from their work via an essay. They were asked to reflect on what their designed artefact told them about the future of journalism.

The future of journalism is. . .

According to my Journalism Design students, the future of journalism: 'is full of possibilities'; 'needs to offer knowledge via an engaging experience'; 'relies on ambitious and revolutionary ideas'; 'is more than telling stories'; 'will never become irrelevant'; 'may even be the start of creating social change amongst audiences'.

Anyone interested in the plight of the news media and its role in society should be encouraged by comments like this. Far from a sense of trepidation about employment, these young people see value and meaning in their future journalistic practice. They talk of wanting to 'lead, innovate and create', of wanting to 'invoke raw feelings', 'to be able to spark thought in audiences' and 'to delve into new and exciting realms'. These are not the reflections of students concerned by news of another round of newsroom job cuts. But these are also aspirations that are unlikely to be satisfied in contemporary news organisations.

What emerges through the essays is a sense that while core journalistic values such as truth, ethics and the public interest are paramount, the practice of journalism needs to accommodate better the needs of audiences and society. There is a strong sense that telling stories and informing the public is not sufficient and, instead, journalism must integrate its practices with people and with other fields of practice. One student observed that journalism itself should not be the focus: 'Instead of asking "what do people want from journalism?", we need to be asking "what do people want?"' Another noted that it was not enough to 'move traditional journalism on to digital platforms; we need to be rewriting the rules of content, production and consumption, without undermining journalistic values'. While there was a recognition that technology provided many opportunities, there was also a sense of caution: 'I am concerned that news outlets will continue to enable personalisation in an effort to compete with social media trends. They should instead be attempting to repair their relationship with consumers to regain trust.' Journalism, in this future vision, has a role and relationship with readers that is distinct from the relationship between social networks and their users.

What also emerged in the essays was the importance of the design process in enabling the students to focus on what was valuable in their ideas and to question some of their own pre-conceived notions about what journalism is. They did not assume that journalistic products were inherently valuable; rather, they saw that, as journalist designers, they must create the value. Part of this new value was linked to the core tenets of journalistic practice, but it also resided in the design of journalistic interactions: how people experience information in virtual or real environments; how they might collaborate with professionals and other citizens; or how to create platforms for specific social groups. Their ideas were not tied to established processes, organisational structures or formats. They were free to imagine users independent of a masthead's audience, and so their designing could concentrate on the junction of journalistic value, technological possibility and the context they defined. Reflecting arguments made by Christensen et al. (2012), Raetzsch (2015) and Boyles (2016), the process encouraged the students to come up with new ideas and new forms of interaction for journalism.

The dominant role of traditional values in students' thinking fits with themes in journalism scholarship: Picard (2010) has suggested that 'efforts to add value should build upon the foundation of journalistic values, not seek to be substitutes for them' (p. 84); and Pavlik (2013) advocates for journalism innovation to be guided by intelligence, freedom of speech, truth and accuracy, and ethics – all key journalistic principles. What interaction design offers is a method for articulating how these values might inform the design of technology.

Design for journalism

Through student projects and the NewsCube project, a practice of Journalism Design begins to emerge. From this perspective,

Journalism Design is about using the methods of interaction design – contextual research, sketching, prototyping, evaluation – as 'tools for thought' (Löwgren and Stolterman 2004) to generate new ideas about how to create new value in journalism. All these projects used a design process to research and imagine a new way of doing journalism: they combined journalistic practice with technology but without the constraint of the newsroom. It meant the prototypes could explore new possibilities.

In this way, Journalism Design sees design as way for journalists to engage proactively with technology. Rather than simply incorporating existing technologies into their practice, journalists can, through design, imagine and create software, devices and interactions that achieve journalistic goals and embody journalistic values. Design is not technology specific, so the approach can be used for any established, emerging or yet-to-be-invented tech. For individuals and news organisations, design offers practical, low-cost and iterative processes that can be tailored to specific goals, situations and audiences. Certainly, such approaches are valuable for developing new journalistic products, but I would suggest that what is equally, if not more, valuable is the use of design as a tool for journalism research. This is because journalism research also needs new ideas.

Schön (1991) points out that there is a 'disturbing tendency for research and practice to follow divergent paths', which means that practitioners and researchers 'have little to say to one another' (p. 308). In journalism, researchers tend to study instances of existing practice, while practitioners do not see the point of journalism studies. The disconnect is recognised widely (for instance, see Skinner et al. 2001; Greenberg 2007; Harcup 2012). Given that the technological challenges facing journalism impact both on scholarship and on industry, there is value in seeing research as an activity of practice. Discussion around practice-led journalism research (Niblock 2012) and the need for research to help shape the future of journalism (Kopper et al. 2000) reinforce this notion. Meanwhile, suggestions that theoretical renewal could emerge from combining disparate approaches (Singer 2008) open a space for new methodological approaches. The future-focused nature of design is a way forward. With its focus on wicked problems, idea generation, and practice-led methods, design research enables journalism scholars to ask questions that address issues of practice. It allows researchers to develop proposals for grappling with challenges in industry. It provides a way of studying those proposals in context and translating theory to practice. It is a way for research and practice to talk to one another.

In this type of research, artefacts are vital. Not only do they embody knowledge, but they represent a new possibility. By putting an artefact – a Journalism Design prototype – into a situation and observing or talking to people about it, it acts as a probe into practice and a tool for reflection on that practice. It enables both the researcher and the user to imagine a new possibility, a different future, and understand not only what might need to change in the present in order to realise that future but also how the present changes what we can imagine for the future: in essence, how to design for tradition and transcendence.

In the previous chapter, I raised the tension between design as exploration and design as product development. Initially the NewsCube was experimental. In keeping with the Research through Design approach, emphasis was on knowledge production, so commercial implications were less important. This meant the prototype could be used to explore possibilities and imagine new ways of working. The feedback on the design suggested scope for exploring alternative shapes or investigating different concepts for tactility and playfulness. However, in the redesigned version these paths were limited to some extent by the requirements of the Walkley Foundation grant. The goal of this phase of the project was less about exploring possibilities and more about scaling a product to a broad user base. This was a goal based in commerce rather than discovery. The tangible outcome of this was not a research prototype but a working beta and a repository of open source code: the key functionality of the NewsCube is available on GitHub via github.com/newscube. This would not have emerged without the goal to build a user base.

Design thinking is a way of using design techniques to create products that customers will buy. But the focus of the work in this book is to use design research to generate new and radical ideas about the future, which may, or may not, be commercially viable. These goals are part of the same continuum, but for the purposes of reimagining journalism practice, it could be useful to put commercial constraints to one side to open space for possibility. In discussing projects with students, I emphasise that they are creating concepts, not products, and to avoid thinking about how to scale, distribute or support their ideas. This type of thinking in the early stages of design tends to hamper their creativity, as ideas are quickly ruled out based on some imaginary business constraint.

Journalism for design

The value of interaction design to journalism practice has been readily apparent. The cases in this book show the value of design in addressing journalistic issues in research and in practice-led student projects. What is less clear is what, if anything, journalism can contribute to interaction design. In my view this is an important challenge of Journalism Design: how to translate journalistic value beyond journalism and into the design of technology. We have only to look at the role of social networks in the recent US presidential election to understand the dangers when traditional journalistic practices are side-lined. So, perhaps there is a role for journalism in the creation of technologies, platforms and interactions not readily associated with news media.

In the NewsCube project, a strong sense of journalistic thinking underpinned the design process. Issues around control, workflow, truth and ethics, for instance, were often addressed by reference to the conventions and constraints of journalistic practice. Similarly, feedback from professional users revealed journalistic approaches to organising content, attitudes to reader involvement in stories, and the newspaper-like tactility of the interface. In student projects, journalistic goals such as informing the public were core design motivations. In these cases, journalism provided the guiding principles and values for the design concepts – journalism informed the design of new technologies.

The internet of things, virtual and augmented reality, robots and tangible interfaces can drive new ways of interacting with and consuming news and information. At the same time, there is a growing recognition that new technologies need to embody human and social goals. Computer scientists are being encouraged to include the needs and perspectives of people in the design of tech. Jacobs (2017) puts the case nicely: 'We need to directly involve affected people in the conception and development of the technologies. We must recognise that community organisers, journalists, educators, educator, ethicists, and everybody else have important perspectives and knowledge essential to building tools and systems' (p. 7). There is a role here for journalistic thinking in creating platforms and interactions that serve the public good.

In this way Journalism Design recognises the contribution journalistic value can make to the design of technologies to serve democratic functions – that journalists' deep craft could be incorporated into the design of new platforms, particularly those that aim to serve the public interest. This may, or may not, involve traditional media. When my JxD students imagine the junction of journalism and technology, it is about remedying the impact of social networks, improving civic participation or exploring emerging technology. Rarely do students investigate issues within established news organisations. This suggests to me that journalism has a distributed and hybrid future: sometimes in the newsroom; sometimes in the community; sometimes in design studios; and sometimes in tech companies.

Next steps

The ideas in this book are a beginning, the first iteration. I have proposed Journalism Design as an emerging area of journalistic research and practice, one that requires many more examples and further study. We need to understand more about practice-led journalism research; the best way to teach interaction design in a journalism curriculum; the possibilities for physical news interactions; and how to design for journalistic values.

The outcomes of research such as this have the potential to disrupt further established journalism practice, but it is important that we investigate the possibilities. Technology, and the way we use it, will continue to evolve. Designing and reimagining is a way for journalists to shape their technological future.

References

Anand, B., 2016. *The content trap: A strategist's guide to digital change.* New York: Random House Publishing Group.

Angus, D., and Doherty, S., 2015. Journalism meets interaction design: An interdisciplinary undergraduate teaching initiative. *Journalism & Mass Communication Educator*, 70 (1), 44–57.

Björgvinsson, E., 2014. Collaborative design and grassroots journalism: Public controversies and controversial publics. In: P. Ehn, E.M. Nilsson, and R. Topgaard, eds. *Making futures: Marginal notes on innovation, design, and democracy*. Cambridge, MA: MIT Press, 227–255.

Blum-Ross, A., Mills, J., Egglestone, P., and Frohlich, D., 2013. Community media and design: Insight Journalism as a method for innovation. *Journal of Media Practice*, 14 (3), 171–192.

Boyles, J.L., 2016. The isolation of innovation: Restructuring the digital newsroom through intrapreneurship. *Digital Journalism*, 4 (2), 229–246.

Christensen, C.M., Skok, D., and Allworth, J., 2012. Breaking news: Mastering the art of disruptive innovation in journalism. *Nieman Reports*, 66 (3), 6–20.

Greenberg, S., 2007. Theory and practice in journalism education. *Journal of Media Practice*, 8 (3), 289–303.

Harcup, T., 2012. Questioning the 'bleeding obvious': What's the point of researching journalism? *Journalism: Theory, Practice & Criticism*, 13 (1), 21–37.

Jacobs, J., 2017. Technology in defense of democracy. *XRDS: Crossroads, The ACM Magazine for Students*, 23 (3), 5–7.

Johnston, J., 2016. *Public relations and the public interest*. London: Routledge.

Kopper, G., Kolthoff, A., and Czepek, A., 2000. Research review: Online journalism – a report on current and continuing research and major questions in the international discussion. *Journalism Studies*, 1 (3), 499–512.

Le Dantec, C.A., 2016. *Designing publics*. Cambridge, MA: MIT Press.

Löwgren, J., and Stolterman, E., 2004. *Thoughtful interaction design: A design perspective on information technology*. Cambridge, MA: MIT Press.

Niblock, S., 2012. Envisioning journalism practice as research. *Journalism Practice*, 6 (4), 497–512.

Pavlik, J.V., 2013. Innovation and the future of journalism. *Digital Journalism*, 1 (2), 181–193.

Picard, R.G., 2010. *Value creation and the future of news organisations*. Barcelona: Formalpress.

Raetzsch, C., 2015. Innovation through practice: Journalism as a structure of public communication. *Journalism Practice*, 9 (1), 65–77.

Schön, D.A., 1991. *The reflective practitioner: How professionals think in action*. 2nd ed. Farnham, England: Ashgate.

Singer, J.B., 2008. Journalism research in the United States: Paradigm shift in a networked world. In: M. Löffelholz and D. Weaver, eds. *Global journalism research: Theories, methods, findings, future*. Malden, MA: Wiley-Blackwell, 145–157.

Skinner, D., Gasher, M.J., and Compton, J., 2001. Putting theory to practice: A critical approach to journalism studies. *Journalism*, 2 (3), 341–360.

Taylor, N., Frohlich, D., Egglestone, P., Marshall, J., Rogers, J., Blum-Ross, A., Mills, J., Shorter, M., and Oliver, P., 2014. *Utilising insight journalism for community technology design*. Presented at the Proceedings of the SIGCHI Conference on Human Factors in Computing Systems, ACM Press, 2995–3004.

Index

Note: Page numbers in *italics* refer to a figure.

Printed in the United States
by Baker & Taylor Publisher Services